Grokking Magento:
Book 1 - Basics & Request Flow

Vinai Kopp

Contents

Chapter 1

Introduction

Welcome to the first book of the *Grokking Magento* series.

About this book

This book series has been a long time dream of mine. I am happy to be able to finally start this project, together with my friend and colleague Ben Marks.

The target audience for this book are experienced PHP developers wanting to learn about the Magento platform.

The book series has three man goals:

1. Help prepare for the Magento Certified Developer Exam (MCD)
2. To be used as a reference for best practices and Magento architecture
3. Give solutions to specific problems in a "developer cookbook" style

The book content follows the Magento Certification Study Group Moderator Kit[1] published by Magento.

---

[1] http://www.magentocommerce.com/certification/moderators-kit

It takes the bare bone exercises and solutions provided by the Study Group Kit and provides insight into the core architecture by researching how a solution may be approached. Then it discusses the example exercise solutions provided with this book.

Along the way, many aspects of the Magento architecture are uncovered, thus providing the background knowledge and mindset required to pass the MCD exam.

Almost as a side effect readers will find they become more efficient and effective as Magento developers.

This first book in the series focuses on the exercises from the Basics and Request Flow section of the Study Group Kit.
It covers the following topics:

- Class name resolution
- How and why class rewrites work
- Application Area Emulation
- The Request Flow Process
- The Front Controller
- Database Based Request Rewrites
- Configuration Based Request Rewrites
- Action Controller Instantiation
- The Action Controller Dispatch Process
- Route Configuration
- Action Controller Rewrites
- Action Controller Flags
- The Event Dispatch Process and Observer Configuration
- The Configuration XML Loading and Merging Process
- Setting, Reading and Saving Configuration Values
- The Magento Application Dispatch Process
- The Store View Selection Process
- Approaches for Multi-Website Setups
- The Customer Session beforeAuthUrl and afterAuthUrl Properties
- Email Template Placeholders and Variables
- Custom Email Template Variables

The Magento Developer Certification Preparation Study Group Moderator Kit

One of the main tools Magento offers to prepare for the Magento Certified Developer exam (in short: MCD) is the *Magento Developer Certification Preparation Study Group Moderator Kit.*
Phew, what a name!

We'll just call it the "Study Group Kit".

The study group kit is good but rather bare-bones. Besides instructions on how to organize and structure meetings, it comes with a bunch of exercises for each of the content sections and some example solutions.
However, for some of the exercises no solutions are provided, and the solutions that do exist only have a few comments in the source code to explain what is happening.

The Study Group Kit really is relying on **you**, or your study group, to dig deep into the Magento source code to figure out how things work exactly.
On one hand this makes sense, since it facilitates learning the ins and outs of the Magento framework.

On the other hand, it may not be the fastest way to learn for everybody, and certainly not the easiest. Also it is easy to miss things.

This book and the others in the *Grokking Magento* series aim to be a guide through the exercises and solutions, providing additional insight while still helping the reader to become accustomed to the Magento core code.

Prerequisites

This book is not a basic introduction to Magento development.
There are many books and online resources available to get a novice Magento developer started with creating custom Magento modules.

This book series expects the reader to have some prior knowledge about Magento.

To gain the most from this book, the reader should be familiar with the following topics:

- Good knowledge of the PHP language
- A solid understanding of object-oriented PHP
- How to create a skeleton Magento module

- The Magento directory structure
- The details of `Varien_Object`'s magic getters and setters[2]

The more context you already have, the more you will benefit from this book.

If you are reading this book as a novice Magento developer, it makes sense to return to this book again later with more knowledge.

You can be sure to gain additional knowledge and better understanding the second time around.

What this book offers

Firstly, this book contains better solutions to the exercises of one section of the MCD study group kit.

What's more, it not only comes with the solution code for the exercises, but also provides extensive documentation for the code in the form of this book.

This book can be used as a reference whenever you want to dig into a specific area of Magento development, independently from being in the process of preparing for the MCD exam.

One of the best skills to develop in order to become a better Magento developer is the ability to read core code.
As everything in life, practice is key. The series also hopes to facilitate building that skill by taking apart core methods, commenting on what code sections do, and putting them into context.

The structure of the chapters

Each exercise is discussed in detail.
First there is a reflection on **real world scenarios**, in which a given exercise might be relevant.

[2]You can find some information on the `Varien_Object` getter capabilities in the addendum to this book.

Some ideas might be a little far-fetched, but I hope to come up with good scenarios that make sense for most cases.
I personally find it a lot easier to think about a problem if I know why I need to solve it. Putting an exercise into context also helps remembering the solution, so the knowledge can be called upon in future projects.

The next part of each chapter is some **background research**.
This part of the chapter is a dive into the Magento core code in order to find out what needs be known to be able to implement a good solution.

Along the way, the discussions might take some detours on related subjects once in a while. This may happen out of two reasons:

1) The content could be part of the certification exam, and there was no better place to talk about it.
2) The content serves to get a bigger picture of how Magento works.

Simply follow along, as the text will be back on the main track towards the exercise solution again in a little while.

Then, after gathering the required architectural information, the actual **solution code** is dissected step by step.

Because the example source code supplied with the study group kit is not free to be shared, all solutions have been developed specifically for this book.

However, it's in the nature of Magento that two solutions for the same problem might be similar to each other.
For example, building an adminhtml grid based on the adminhtml widget blocks simply has to be done in a specific way to get the desired outcome.

We recommend you take the time to compare the solutions provided by this book and the study group kit to gain additional insights, if possible.
However, of course this book may also be used on its own, without a copy of the study group kit.

Since the current version of the MCD exams is based on Magento CE 1.7.0.2, that is also the version used for this companion material.
At the time of writing, the current version of Magento 1 CE is 1.8.1.0.
If the exam is updated, we will be updating this book, too.
Almost everything in this book also applies to newer versions of Magento 1, too.

To summarize, this series hopes to supply the "meat" to the "bare-bones" study group kit, in addition to serve as a reference, by providing

- Solutions to all exercises
- Discussion of the Magento architecture in regards to the exercises
- Discussion of the exercise solution code

How to use this material

Obviously, this work is meant to be read. Its purpose is to help get you ready to pass the Magento certification, or to solve problems during Magento development.

Reading this book is only one step. While reading the pages, you should do it in a way that helps you remember all the information.

Here are a few tips that help me tremendously when learning new things.

- After reading a section, put the book aside and try to implement the solution on your own. If you get stuck, read the chapter again up where you got stuck, and then continue to work on your own.

- While the text is discussing parts of the core, follow along through the source code in your IDE.
  Because the core code sometimes is quite verbose, only relevant parts will be included in the chapters. Going through the real code will give you context, and help you build your core code reading skill.

- Don't rush. If you can, approach reading this book in the spirit of relaxed exploration.

- Take breaks. Your brain will probably be able to absorb much more information if you take a 20 minute break after each exercise. Do not plan to cover more than two or three exercises per day.

- A day or so after completing an exercise using this book, compare this solution with the one supplied by the study group kit. Reading more code that does the same thing will help anchor the information in your long term memory.
  Some solutions might differ, and you may gain additional insights by looking at "a second opinion".

- If you find yourself having difficulties understanding a concept or some code, don't just push through.
  Instead, make a list of things you need to know, and then fill those gaps, before returning to the chapter and reading on.
  Filling the gaps might mean re-reading a previous chapter, visiting the PHP manual[3], or looking at / asking questions on the Magento StackExchange site[4].

Core Code Samples

Often, parts of the Magento core code will be discussed in the chapters.
The samples in the book might be abbreviated in order to make them easier to read.

For example, any calls to `Varien_Profiler::start()` and `Varien_Profiler::stop()` will be removed.

But also larger sections might be taken away to emphasise the main concept the book content is trying to transport.

Please don't be surprised when you find things to be somewhat different when comparing code in the book to the actual sources.

Any code in the book will contain all relevant information you need in order to follow along.

Exercise Solution Code

The exercise solution code referred to in the chapters can be downloaded from shop.vinaikopp.com/grokking-magento/pk342e/[5] If you purchased this book as an ePub from shop.vinaikopp.com[6] the code is also available as an additional download with your order.

Please respect the work that has gone into creating the book and the code and instead of distributing the it, encourage others to purchase their own copy.

---

[3]http://php.net/en/manual
[4]http://magento.stackexchange.com/
[5]https://shop.vinaikopp.com/grokking-magento/pk342e/
[6]https://shop.vinaikopp.com/

Magento Trivia

There are aspects of Magento that knowing about is absolutely useless for real work projects. They also are not required to pass the MCD exam.

There is a certain type of developer personality who enjoys that kind of thing nevertheless (me included).
For that reason, the book will sometimes contain such information.
In that case it will be marked as **Magento Trivia**, so you can choose to skip it if you want to.

Acknowledgements

First and foremost, a big **Thank You** to the Magento developer community.

There are so many excellent developers from whom I have learned so much.
Regardless what anyone might think about the product itself, the Magento developer community is first class!

Second, thank you Magento for creating such a powerful and flexible platform, and for releasing it as open source! Without you, there would be no Magento eco system - I can't even imagine a world like that.

Third, thank you to my mentors and friends from without and within Magento.
All of you have played a vital role at one point during my continued journey of learning Magento. I especially want to include a shout out to the following

- Vitaliy Golomoziy - you inspired me by showing how deep broad understanding can be.
- Lee Saferite - you taught me that learning to read and understand core code is not only possible but is an essential skill.
- Susie Sedlacek - you taught me about the business game, and did so in a good way.

There are many other people within Magento that I have come to think of as friends more then colleagues. Thank you for being you.

A special thank you to all Ukrainian members of the Magento offices and everybody of the Ukrainian Magento community I have the privilege to know.
You inspire me to grow and expand continuously, not only as a developer. I value your passion and honesty.

Also, I thank all of the students from all the trainings I've lead over the years. Your questions challenge me and your curiosity and participation keeps my love for my work alive. What's more, you make every class a fun experience. Thank you!

Thanks to all MagentoRunning buddies, in particular Brent Peterson and Thomas Fleck. Looking forward to our next sweaty adventures!

A big thank you to Sandro Kopp for designing and drawing the lovely cover art (it is a silver fern frond if you where wondering).

And finally: thank you to my family - you are my sunshine.

Chapter 2

Development Environment

How to set up a proper Magento Development environment isn't included in the Study Group Kit.

However, a good moderator should point out what will be needed to set up a decent development environment during the first meeting.

PHP

Magento 1 officially still supports the ancient version 5.2 of PHP, but consider running at least PHP 5.3.6 since it contains many useful features.
Magento has provided download patches to support PHP 5.4 for older versions of Magento, too, so there is no real reason to still use PHP 5.2.
Many community developers are using PHP 5.5 already with Magento in order to take advantage of the many new features without experiencing any real issues.

Using an OpCode Cache like the Zend Optimizer or APC is also highly recommended. Magento is a heavy weight application, and every little improvement helps.

Installing and learning to use xdebug[1] (or the Zend debugger if you are using Zend Server) is one of the most valuable things a PHP developer can do.
So in case you aren't familiar with it, start now.

---

[1] http://xdebug.org/

IDE

Currently the IDE most Magento developers favor is PhpStorm[2] in combination with the
Magicento[3] plugin.
This makes for a highly efficient Magento development setup.
A single developer licence for PhpStorm is very cheap when compared to other commercial
IDE products.

There are free alternatives of course: Eclipse[4] and Eclipse Magento Plugin[5], or Netbeans[6]
most prominently.
Both IDEs are open source, free, and excellent products. However, working with them isn't
as smooth and effortless as with PhpStorm, and they tend to be slower.

Sublime Text 2[7] with SublimePHPIntel[8] is a combination many developers love, however
it can't match the amount of support a developer gets from a full IDE (at least currently).

There are other IDEs and editors (Zend Studio, Aptana, Komodo etc), however they are
far less popular and seem to be slowly losing ground in the marketplace.

That said, it certainly is possible to develop Magento extensions using nothing but a text
editor.
However, only a person with superhuman powers could claim to be as efficient that way as
with an IDE.

Testing Framework Integrations

Since the first release of PHPUnit[9] a lot has happened in the world of PHP testing.
It is a complex topic, however everybody who gets into the habit of writing tests doesn't
want to go back.

It is very possible to write tests for custom Magento modules with plain PHPUnit.

---

[2] http://www.jetbrains.com/phpstorm/
[3] http://magicento.com/
[4] http://projects.eclipse.org/projects/tools.pdt
[5] http://eclipse.snowdog.pl/
[6] https://netbeans.org/features/php/
[7] http://www.sublimetext.com/2
[8] https://github.com/jotson/SublimePHPIntel
[9] http://phpunit.de/manual/current/en/index.html

However, because Magento uses many static method calls and practically violates the Law of Demeter[10] in almost every method, it is sometimes not a straightforward process. Either large amounts of objects need to be mocked, or complex fixtures need to be created.

Several integrations have been developed to help writing tests for Magento.

The most well-known one is EcomDev_PHPUnit[11]. Its outstanding feature is the excellent support for creating fixtures in yaml files.
Besides that it also offers many assertions and workarounds to make the Magento framework more test-friendly.
Check out the development branch if you choose to try it out.

The Mage_Test[12] integration is a much more lightweight PHPUnit integration. It provides basic support and help to make Magento testable.
It is under active, albeit slow, development. Check out the development branch to see what is going on. However, if you already are familiar with PHPUnit you might feel quite at ease with it.

The project magetest.org[13] aims to provide a set of unit-tests for the Magento core. It might be useful as a smoke-test. For the Magento testing integration it uses EcomDev_PHPUnit.

The BDD framework Behat[14] and its Magento integration BehatMage[15] are different. It doesn't aim to provide unit test features, but instead enables users to test business specifications written in a human readable language known as Gherkin. Behat itself is getting quite mature, but the Magento integration is still lacking some features.
For example testing multi-site instances with separate domains isn't possible out of the box.

The PHPSpec2[16] functional testing framework is another framework not based on PHPUnit. It features the semi-automatic generation of tests. However, the standard mocking library Prophecy doesn't play well with Magento's magic setter and getter methods, so it's always necessary to fall back to Mockery (or even PHPUnit) for stubs and mocks.
There is a project to integrate Magento with PHPSpec2 called MageSpec[17], but once again development isn't going very quickly.

---

[10]http://en.wikipedia.org/wiki/Law_of_Demeter
[11]https://github.com/EcomDev/EcomDev_PHPUnit
[12]https://github.com/MageTest/Mage-Test
[13]http://www.magetest.org/
[14]http://behat.org/
[15]https://github.com/MageTest/BehatMage
[16]http://www.phpspec.net/
[17]https://github.com/MageTest/MageSpec

A relatively new testing framework is codeception[18].
It follows a similar approach to testing as Behat, but as far as I'm aware of there is no toolset for Magento available yet.

Basically all tools to run functional tests can be used with Magento, too.
They either remote control a browser window (for example using Selenium or Sahi) or using a headless browser (currently the phantomjs based tools are very popular).

Choosing the right tool for the job is left to the reader, since there is no "one size fits all" recommendation.

---

[18]http://codeception.com/

Chapter 3

Exercise: Rewrite the sales/order model, add the group ID as an email template variable

Original task description

The original task description from the study group kit for this exercise is as follows:

> Rewrite the sales/order model to add the customer group model as an email template variable in the sendNewOrderEmail() method, so the group code can be added to the email using {{var customer_group.getCode()}}.

Overview

This chapter discusses the following topics in the research section and the examination of the exercise solution:

- The method sendNewOrderEmail() of the sales/order model

- Using `core/app_emulation` and its benefits over `setCurrentStore()`
- Email template variables and placeholders
- Custom CMS and email template directives
- How class name resolution is done and how model rewrites work

Scenario

Imagine that for some reason the store owner wants to include the customer group name in the new order email.

Maybe they would like to add conditional blocks in to the template, so they are able to display different promotions to different groups.

Research

Let's start by having a look at the method in question:
`Mage_Sales_Model_Order::sendNewOrderEmail()`.

The method is quite long. A pity it doesn't follow the good old rule of thumb that each method should completely fit on the screen.

For reference purposes it is a good idea if you open the method in your IDE, while we break it up and examine it section by section here.

Along the way we will examine different areas of the Magento core code that make the process of sending emails work, but also are useful in other contexts.

Switching Areas: core/app_emulation

The first interesting part is at the beginning, where the store is pseudo-switched to the store view of the order.

The essential section of code in regards to this is about 10 lines into the method:

```
// Start store emulation process
$appEmulation = Mage::getSingleton('core/app_emulation');
$initialEnvironmentInfo = $appEmulation->startEnvironmentEmulation($storeId);
```

The original environment will then be restored later using
$appEmulation->stopEnvironmentEmulation($initialEnvironmentInfo).

Let's have a quick detour and look at what this environment emulation is about.

```
public function startEnvironmentEmulation(
    $storeId,
    $area = Mage_Core_Model_App_Area::AREA_FRONTEND,
    $emulateSroreInlineTranslation = false
) {
    if (is_null($area)) {
        $area = Mage_Core_Model_App_Area::AREA_FRONTEND;
    }
    if ($emulateSroreInlineTranslation) {
        $initialTranslateInline = $this->_emulateInlineTranslation(
            $storeId, $area
        );
    } else {
        $initialTranslateInline = $this->_emulateInlineTranslation();
    }
    $initialDesign = $this->_emulateDesign($storeId, $area);
    // Current store needs to be changed right before
    // locale change and after design change
    Mage::app()->setCurrentStore($storeId);
    $initialLocaleCode = $this->_emulateLocale($storeId, $area);

    $initialEnvironmentInfo = new Varien_Object();
    $initialEnvironmentInfo->setInitialTranslateInline($initialTranslateInline)
        ->setInitialDesign($initialDesign)
        ->setInitialLocaleCode($initialLocaleCode);

    return $initialEnvironmentInfo;
}
```

The method call takes care that the following aspects of Magento are set as if the request had been for the specified store:

- The area
- The theme configuration
- the locale
- the current store

To summarize, using `core/app_emulation` is more complete than just calling the common `Mage::app()->setCurrentStore($storeId)`.

Going back to the `sendNewOrderEmail()` method, what happens while the order's store is being emulated?

```
$paymentBlock = Mage::helper('payment')->getInfoBlock($this->getPayment())
    ->setIsSecureMode(true);
$paymentBlock->getMethod()->setStore($storeId);
$paymentBlockHtml = $paymentBlock->toHtml();
```

The payment info block is rendered into a variable **$paymentBlockHtml**. After that, the environment emulation is ended.

Ask yourself, "why is the environment emulation needed?"

Usually the store ID set on an order matches the current store while the order is placed. But if the order is being placed using the Admin panel, the current store is the admin store view. The adminhtml theme is being used, together with the admin user's locale configuration.
But of course the payment information in an order email should match the customer's settings, for whom the order is being created.
For that reason the settings are switched accordingly during the payment info block rendering using the app emulation.

Email template placeholders and variables

Moving on further in the `sendNewOrderEmail()` method, we don't need to discuss the next few lines in detail.
They simply get configuration settings to initialize the `core/email_template_mailer` instance.
The relevant part for us is towards the end of the method, where the template variables are specified:

```
$mailer->setTemplateParams(array(
        'order'        => $this,
        'billing'      => $this->getBillingAddress(),
        'payment_html' => $paymentBlockHtml
    )
);
$mailer->send();
```

The array values will be accessible in the email templates by using `{{var ...}}` placeholders referencing the array keys passed to the `setTemplateParams()` method. One example for such a placeholder directive could be `{{var payment_html}}`, which would include the rendered payment information block into the email.

Note that the template parameters are specified directly before the email is sent.

Please note that we are currently **not** discussing Magento's .phtml template files!
This section of the book is about the template system used for transactional emails and CMS content.
Only the name *template* is the same, but otherwise these two are quite distinct!
More information on theme template files can be found in the next book in this series, "Rendering & Widgets".

According to best practices, it would be ideal if we could add the new customer group template variable using an event observer.
But looking at the methods
`Mage_Core_Model_Email_Template_Mailer::setTemplateParams()` and `send()` doesn't reveal any useful events.
There don't seem to be any earlier ones, either, as searching for the string "`dispatchEvent`" within the class turns up nothing.

We will have to look further for the best way to implement our customization.
Lets continue to analyze how the template variables are processed further.

The `core/email_template_mailer` class delegates to `core/email_template`, more specifically, to its `sendTransactional()` method.
This in turn calls its `send()` method, and there, finally, the template variables are processed.

```
$text = $this->getProcessedTemplate($variables, true);
```

The class `Mage_Core_Model_Email_Template_Filter` is not only used for email templates. The CMS filter class also makes heavy use of it when rendering CMS blocks and pages.

It is worth taking another detour to look at the way variables can be accessed in templates.

The key method is `Varien_Filter_Template::_getVariable()`.

This method implements all the different ways how template placeholder directives can be used to access the template variables.

```
protected function _getVariable($value, $default='{no_value_defined}')
{
    $tokenizer = new Varien_Filter_Template_Tokenizer_Variable();
    $tokenizer->setString($value);
    $stackVars = $tokenizer->tokenize();
```

The value passed to the method is the content part of a template {{var ...}} placeholder directive.
For example, for a placeholder {{var foo}}, the argument variable **$value** would be set to foo.

This value is the tokenized, that is *split*, using the dot character as a separator. This character is hardcoded in the `Varien_Filter_Template_Tokenizer_Variable` class.

Then each of the tokens are analyzed in a **for** loop.
This is required because tokens can be chained, as we will see further below.
Each token that is resolved will update the token stack to the latest value.
This continues until the full stack of tokens is resolved, and the final replacement value has been determined.

```
        $result = $default;
        $last = 0;
        for($i = 0; $i < count($stackVars); $i ++) {
          if ($i == 0 && isset($this->_templateVars[$stackVars[$i]['name']])) {
            // Getting of template value
            $stackVars[$i]['variable'] =& $this->_templateVars[$stackVars[$i]['name']];
          } else if (isset($stackVars[$i-1]['variable'])
                && $stackVars[$i-1]['variable'] instanceof Varien_Object) {
            // If object calling methods or getting properties
            if($stackVars[$i]['type'] == 'property') {
              $caller = "get" . uc_words($stackVars[$i]['name'], '');
              if(is_callable(array($stackVars[$i-1]['variable'], $caller))) {
                // If specified getter for this property
                $stackVars[$i]['variable'] = $stackVars[$i-1]['variable']->$caller();
              } else {
                $stackVars[$i]['variable'] = $stackVars[$i-1]['variable']
```

```
                                         ->getData($stackVars[$i]['name']);
            }
        } else if ($stackVars[$i]['type'] == 'method') {
            // Calling of object method
            if (is_callable(
                    array($stackVars[$i-1]['variable'], $stackVars[$i]['name'])
                ) || substr($stackVars[$i]['name'],0,3) == 'get'
            ) {
                $stackVars[$i]['variable'] =
                    call_user_func_array(array($stackVars[$i-1]['variable'],
                                               $stackVars[$i]['name']),
                                         $stackVars[$i]['args']);
            }
        }
        $last = $i;
    }
}

if(isset($stackVars[$last]['variable'])) {
    // If value for construction exists set it
    $result = $stackVars[$last]['variable'];
}
return $result;
}
```

To be honest, it isn't the most easy to understand piece of code.
An approach that tends to work well with code like that is to analyze it bit by bit to make it more digestible.

The most interesting part is within the **for** loop, where the code evaluates the type of the tokens (aka parts of the variable name), and fetches the value to replace it with.

Each token can be one of two things: either it is a predefined name, or it is a property or method of a `Varien_Object`.

To give some context: the method _getVariable() is called from several places (as you can confirm by a quick search over the core code):

- `Mage_Core_Model_Template_Filter::varDirective()`
- `Varien_Filter_Template::varDirective()`
- `Varien_Filter_Template::dependDirective()`
- `Varien_Filter_Template::ifDirective()`

- Varien_Filter_Template::_getIncludeParameters() (which is called, amongst others, from htmlescapeDirective())

Each of the methods whose name ends in `Directive` processes a matching directive that can be used in the template text.

For example, {{if ...}} will be processed by the `ifDirective()` method.
The **$value** passed to the method above is the placeholder directive's content string.

Since assigned variables can be used in a variety of contexts, it is quite useful to know how to access variable contents in email and CMS templates.

Here are some examples of valid variable template declarations so we know what we are looking for while reading the `_getVariable()` method.

Variables with plain text or HTML content:

- {{var payment_html}}
- {{htmlescape var=$payment_html}}

These would be the predifined names checked first in the **for** loop.

Properties of objects contained in variables can be accessed using a dot as a separator in a variety of ways.

Consider the following two variables from the current exercise:

- {{var order.customer_name}}
- {{var order.getCustomerName()}}

If such a token value "returns" a `Varien_Object` instance, further calls may be chained:

- {{var order.billing_address.getCity()}}
- {{var order.getBillingAddress().city}}
- {{htmlescape var=$order.billing_address().city}}

This kind of method or property chaining to access object properties can be used everywhere `_getVariable()` is used.

Please read over the `_getVariable()` method one more time for each of the given examples, and step through the code in your mind, resolving each of the tokens one at a time.
I'm sure after this brain exercise the method will be quite clear.

Custom email template directives

Let's go a bit deeper into the subject of email and CMS page directives, even if it's not directly relevant for the current exercise.
So far this chapter only talked about the {{var ...}} and {{htmlescape var=...}} directives.

It is quite easy to implement custom directives, for example {{customergroup}}, to output the current customer group name.

The base functionality for this is inherited from the class
Varien_Filter_Template::filter().
Whenever a placeholder is found, the class checks if there is a method matching the placeholder name, followed by the word Directive.

The {{custmrgrp}} placeholder for example would cause the filter class to check for a method custmrgrpDirective().
Note that no underscores are allowed in the placeholder names.
The regular expression that is used to match the placeholders is
/{{([a-z]{0,10})(.*?)}}/si.

The method implementing a directive receives the captured parts from the regular expression as an argument.

Using $params = $this->_getIncludeParameters($matches[2]) any arguments to the directive can be easily parsed.
Any parameter values starting with a $ will automatically be evaluated using the _getVariable() method discussed above.

The placeholder will then be replaced by the string value the directive returns.

For example, a directive for the placeholder
{{custmrgrp id=$order.getCustomerGroupId()}} could look like this:

```
public function custmrgrpDirective($matches)
{
    $params = $this->_getIncludeParameters($matches[2]);
    if (isset($params['id'])) {
        $groupId = (int)$params['id'];
    } else {
        $groupId = Mage::getSingleton('customer/session')
                        ->getCustomerGroupId();
    }
```

```
    $group = Mage::getModel('customer/group')->load($groupId);
    return $group->getCode();
}
```

The method will render the code of the customer group whose ID was specified as an argument using the `id` parameter.
If no group ID was specified, the current customer group is used.

The directive is called `custmrgrp` instead of `customergroup` because the regular expression matching the placeholders allows for a maximum of 10 characters as the placeholder name.

The example placeholder used above,
`{{custmrgrp id=$order.getCustomerGroupId()}}`, uses the parameter `$order` which is available in the new order emails.

There are several options available to let Magento know you want a custom filter class to be used.

For CMS pages and blocks you can either configure a class rewrite for the `cms/template_filter` model, or you can specify the class using the config XPath `global/cms/page/tempate_filter` and `global/cms/page/tempate_filter`.[1]

To make your custom directive available in email templates you need to rewrite the model `core/email_template_filter`.

Enough of the template variable detour! Time to get back on track and figure out how to specify the customer group as a template variable.

Since we did not find any matching events, we need to fall back to a class rewrite of the `sales/order` class.
That is the only way we will be able to add our custom logic to the `sendNewOrderEmail()` method.

Solution

The example solution code can be found in the extension `Meeting02_RewriteOrder`.

---

[1] The typo **tempate** instead of **template** in the config path is Magento's, not mine.

Why class rewrites work

All Magento developers know *how* to specify a model rewrite in configuration XML, but few know *why* that works, and that is what is needed during the MCD exam.

Magento uses factory methods. These factory methods take a string as their first argument. This string is then mapped to a real PHP class name by a series of steps consisting mostly of looking up values from config XML. This process is known as **class name resolution**.

Let's go through a concrete example by having a look at the configuration XML which is necessary to declare a rewrite for the `sales/order` model, and then see how it is processed by Magento.

```xml
<config>
    <global>
        <models>
            <sales>
                <rewrite>
                    <order>Meeting02_RewriteOrder_Model_Sales_Order</order>
                </rewrite>
            </sales>
        </models>
    </global>
</config>
```

In Magento, to create a fresh instance of a new model, usually the `Mage::getModel()` factory method is called.

```php
$order = Mage::getModel('sales/order');
```

Let's have a look at the factory method itself.

```php
public static function getModel($modelClass = '', $arguments = array())
{
    return self::getConfig()->getModelInstance($modelClass, $arguments);
}
```

Note: there is an optional second argument which will be passed to the constructor if present. This feature is shared by most of Magento's factory methods.

The call is delegated to `Mage_Core_Model_Config::getModelInstance()`.

```
public function getModelInstance($modelClass='', $constructArguments=array())
{
    $className = $this->getModelClassName($modelClass);
    // ... further code omitted for now ...
}
```

The class name resolution is delegated to the method getModelClassName().

```
public function getModelClassName($modelClass)
{
    $modelClass = trim($modelClass);
    if (strpos($modelClass, '/')===false) {
        return $modelClass;
    }
    return $this->getGroupedClassName('model', $modelClass);
}
```

The condition in this method has the consequence that if you pass a regular PHP class name to Mage::getModel(), it will abort the lookup process and simply use the name as-is.

This means that for any rewrites to take effect, the class alias (with the /) needs to be used.

For example:

```
// Class rewrites apply if present
$order = Mage::getModel('sales/order');

// Class rewrites will be ignored
$order = Mage::getModel('Mage_Sales_Model_Order');
```

The method Mage_Core_Model_Config::getGroupedClassName() contains the generic code for class name resolution, regardless of the type of object being instantiated.

All other factory methods for helpers, blocks and so on use it as well. Whenever you question why a rewrite isn't working, this is the place to go and see what is actually happening.

Let's start by looking at each part in order.

```
public function getGroupedClassName($groupType, $classId, $groupRootNode=null)
{
```

```
if (empty($groupRootNode)) {
    $groupRootNode = 'global/'.$groupType.'s';
}
```

The first argument is the object type, which is one of `model`, `block`, or `helper`.
The second argument is the string that was specified as an argument to the factory method,
for example `sales/order`.
We know it contains a `/` since that is confirmed in the preceding methods.
The third argument is not used in the core. It could be used to tell the method to do the
class name resolution by looking at configuration in a custom branch of XML.

In the code section displayed above the variable **`$groupRootNode`** is set to point to the
XML configuration branch for the specified object type.
Models will be resolved using configuration in `global/models`, block configuration will be
in `global/blocks` and helpers will be found under `global/helpers`.

Note the 's' that is appended to the group type. It is a common mistake to forget the
plural form there.

Let's move on.

```
$classArr = explode('/', trim($classId));
$group = $classArr[0];
$class = !empty($classArr[1]) ? $classArr[1] : null;

if (isset($this->_classNameCache[$groupRootNode][$group][$class])) {
    return $this->_classNameCache[$groupRootNode][$group][$class];
}
```

This is one of the most important steps: the class alias is exploded on the `/`.
The string `sales/order` is split into `sales` and `order`. Let's clarify some naming conventions before we continue.

Part	Name	Variable	Sometimes also called
model	**Object Type**	$groupType	
sales/order	**Class Alias**	$classId	**Class ID** or **Factory Name**
sales	**Class Group**	$group	
order	**Class Suffix**	$class	**The-Part-After-The-Slash**

Part	Name	Variable	Sometimes also called
Mage_Sales_Model	**Class Prefix**		See below for what this is

Table 3.1: Naming conventions during class name resolution

I will stick to the identifiers under the **Name** column, but at Magento meetups or conferences you might also hear the parts called by other names.

As you can see, the `core/config` class which is doing the resolution utilizes a lookup cache. Once a class alias is resolved, following requests for the same alias no longer need to go through the whole process again.

```
$config = $this->_xml->global->{$groupType.'s'}->{$group};

// First - check maybe the entity class was rewritten
$className = null;
if (isset($config->rewrite->$class)) {
    $className = (string)$config->rewrite->$class;
```

The actual configuration for the specified class group is stored in the variable `$config`. In our example case, `sales/order`, that would be the entire configuration contained within the `<sales>` node.

```
<config>
    <global>
        <models>
            <sales>
                ...
            </sales>
        </models>
    </global>
</config>
```

Or, in Magento's simplified XPath notation: `global/models/sales`.

Please Note: the first real configuration lookup to determine the real PHP class name is done here!

To continue our example: if the node **global/models/sales/rewrite/order** exists, its value is assigned to the variable **$className** and will be used as the PHP class name. In this case class resolution is complete!

This is why a class rewrite in XML uses the following structure:

```
<config>
  <global>
    <[Object Type]s>
      <[Class Group]>
        <rewrite>
          <[Class Suffix]>The_Php_Class_Name_That_Is_Used</[Class Suffix]>
        </rewrite>
      </[Class Group]>
    </[Object Type]s>
  </global>
</config>
```

Or, in our concrete example case, a class rewrite for **sales/order** would need to be specified as follows.

```
<config>
    <global>
        <models>
            <sales>
                <rewrite>
                    <order>Meeting02_RewriteOrder_Model_Sales_Order</order>
                </rewrite>
            </sales>
        </models>
    </global>
</config>
```

Class name resolution is not applied recursively, so it is **not possible** to rewrite a rewritten class and have both rewrites be in effect.
But what happens if no rewrite exists for the class alias in question?

```
    } else {
    /**
     * Backwards compatibility for pre-MMDB extensions.
```

```
  * In MMDB release resource nodes <..._mysql4> were renamed
  * to <..._resource>. So < deprecatedNode> is left to keep
  * name of previously used nodes, that still may be used by
  * non-updated extensions.
  */
if ($config->deprecatedNode) {
  $deprecatedNode = $config->deprecatedNode;
  $configOld = $this->_xml->global->{$groupType.'s'}->$deprecatedNode;
  if (isset($configOld->rewrite->$class)) {
    $className = (string) $configOld->rewrite->$class;
  }
}
}
```

Luckily we get a nice comment. To understand it, we need to remember that this method is not only used for models, blocks and helpers, but also for resource model class name resolution.

Magento 1.6 introduced a full database abstraction layer called MMDB, I guess which stands for **Magento Multi DataBase**.
(They also published a nice PDF on MMDB[2] at the time.)

While doing so, they unified the resource model structure within all modules, and renamed all **resource class groups**. [3]

Module	Magento 1.0 - 1.5	Magento 1.6 +
Mage_Catalog	catalog_resource_eav_mysql4	catalog_resource
Mage_Customer	customer_entity	customer_resource
Mage_Newsletter	newsletter_mysql4	newsletter_resource

Table 3.2: Examples of MMDB resource class group changes

As you can see, since Magento 1.6 all resource class group names follow the same convention.

---

[2]http://www.magentocommerce.com/images/uploads/RDBMS_Guide.pdf

[3]**Resource class group** is a new term. It would lead us too far astray from the actual exercise to go into more depth here. For now please refer to the addendum Class Name Resolution Steps for further information.

Assume a rewrite would have been specified for the `customer/address` resource model in a Magento version before 1.6.
The configuration path would have had to be:

`global/models/customer_entity/rewrite/address`

With Magento 1.6 the path changed to

`global/models/customer_resource/rewrite/address`

Any modules using the old path would break. For that reason, a new node was introduced: `<deprecatedNode>`.
It contains the old, pre-MMDB, resource model class group of each module.

If no regular rewrite for a class is found, the configuration model checks if a rewrite for the old name is present (see the code block above).

Class name resolution continued

We examined the code responsible for class rewrites, but there still is a little remainder of the `getGroupedClassName()` method left.
Instead of finishing here, let's continue the exploration, even if it doesn't directly apply to the current exercise.
It is definitely useful to know, MCD exam-relevant, and not very long.

Back to the previous question, what happens if no rewrite exists for the class alias being resolved?

```
// Second - if entity is not rewritten then use class prefix to form class name
if (empty($className)) {
    if (!empty($config)) {
        $className = $config->getClassName();
    }
    if (empty($className)) {
        $className = 'mage_'.$group.'_'.$groupType;
    }
    if (!empty($class)) {
        $className .= '_'.$class;
```

```
        }
        $className = uc_words($className);
    }
```

In the code block the configuration model tries to establish a **Class Prefix**, onto which it appends the **class suffix**, to complete the class name resolution.

First it checks for the value returned by the method `Mage_Core_Model_Config_Element::getClassName()`. In effect it returns the value of a child node `<class>` or `<model>` of the class group configuration.

For the class group `sales` the configuration of the class prefix will be at `global/models/sales/class` or `global/model/sales/model`.[4]

It might be confusing that the node name is `<class>`, however, the node value is never a PHP class - it is the class prefix only!
Bad naming choices like this one is part of the reason for Magento's reputation of being difficult to learn.

```
<global>
    <models>
        <sales>
            <class>Mage_Sales_Model</class>
        </sales>
    </model>
</global>
```

Note: The class prefix is prepended directly to the **$class** variable without removing whitespace. Hence the following creates an invalid class name containing whitespace:

```
<class>
    Mage_Sales_Model
</class>
```

If `getClassName()` returns empty, the method `getGroupedClassName()` falls back to constructing a default class prefix.

```
$className = 'mage_'.$group.'_'.$groupType;
```

[4]In practice `<class>` is always used by Magento developers to specify a class prefix. Better stick to that convention unless there is a good reason not to.

The consequence is that core developers can get away without specifying a class prefix for their modules.

We on the other hand, as part of the developer community working outside the Mage namespace, have to always specify a class group and prefix in our modules.

Finishing up, let's examine the last few lines of getGroupedClassName().

```
$this->_classNameCache[$groupRootNode][$group][$class] = $className;
return $className;
}
```

Not much to say about these two lines, except that the result of the class name resolution is stored in the **$_classNameCache** property to speed up future lookups during the current request. The the result is returned and the method is complete.

To complete this sub-section, here is the XML that specifies the class rewrite for the exercise at hand.

```
<config>
    <global>
        <models>
            <sales>
                <rewrite>
                    <order>Meeting02_RewriteOrder_Model_Sales_Order</order>
                </rewrite>
            </sales>
        </models>
    </global>
</config>
```

With this bit of configuration in place, the sales/order class alias resolves to Meeting02_RewriteOrder_Model_Sales_Order instead of the original Mage_Sales_Model_Order.

Using the module name in the object type directory (that is, ...Model_Sales_Order instead of simply ...Model_Order helps organize the folder structure in our module. Following this convention makes it possible to see at a glance which classes in our *Model* directory are originals and which are rewrites.[5]

---

[5]Very handy for example when a module rewrites more than one Data helper and maybe also contains its own Data helper.

Adding the custom email template variable

According to best practices we should not copy a full method from a parent class when doing a rewrite, since that compromises the ability to upgrade. If the method changes in a future version, those changes would be masked by our copy in the rewrite target class. Instead, we should inject our logic before or after calling the parent method.

The next example would be following best practices.

```
public function sendNewOrderEmail()
{
    $this->_addOurCustomTemplateVariable();
    return parent::sendNewOrderEmail();
}
```

Unfortunately, we can't do that in this case. The piece of code we want to change is buried deep in the middle of the parent method.

```
public function sendNewOrderEmail()
{
    // ... a bunch of code ...
    $mailer->setTemplateParams(array(
            'order'         => $this,
            'billing'       => $this->getBillingAddress(),
            'payment_html' => $paymentBlockHtml
        )
    );
    // ... more code ...
}
```

In cases such as this there is no other way than copying the full method to our rewritten class and adding our logic in there directly.
Here is the piece of code including our customization:

```
    $mailer->setTemplateParams(array(
            'order' => $this,
            'billing' => $this->getBillingAddress(),
            'payment_html' => $paymentBlockHtml,
            'customer_group' => $this->_getCustomerGroup()
        )
    );
```

The method to fetch the customer group model is not part of the native order model; we need to implement that ourselves.

```
/**
 * @return Mage_Customer_Model_Group
 */
protected function _getCustomerGroup()
{
    /** @var Mage_Customer_Model_Resource_Group_Collection $groups */
    $groups = Mage::helper('customer')->getGroups();
    $groupId = $this->getCustomerGroupId();
    $group = $groups->getItemById($groupId);
    if (! $group) {
        $group = Mage::getModel('customer/group')->load($groupId);
    }
    return $group;
}
```

The customer helper class method `Mage_Customer_Helper_Data::getGroups()` returns a collection containing all customer groups with an ID larger than 0.
The group with the ID 0 is a special group for guests, that is, not logged in customers.

If the order was placed as a guest, **$this->getCustomerGroupId()** will return 0.
Because of that it is not guaranteed that the collection will contain the needed group.
If that is that case, then **$group** will be **null**, and the customer group model will have to be instantiated and loaded individually.

The reason for trying to get the customer group out of the helper's collection first is that we might be able to avoid an extra database query. Since other parts of Magento also use the helper's **getGroups()** method, and because helpers in Magento are always realized as singletons, the group already might be pre-loaded.

Chapter 4

Exercise: Redirect to / if the home page is accessed directly by CMS page identifier

Original task description

The original task description from the study group kit for this exercise is as follows:

> Create an observer that redirects the visitor to the base URL if the CMS home page URL key is accessed directly (i.e. /home -> /).

Overview

This chapter discusses the following topics in the research section and the examination of the exercise solution:

- CMS page url identifiers
- The Request Flow process
- The Front Controller

- The Standard router
- Database based request rewrites
- Configuration based request rewrites
- The action controller dispatch process
- Action controller flags
- The event dispatch process and observer configuration

Scenario

Having the exact same content accessible on two distinct URLs is rated as duplicate content by Google. For that reason it makes sense to restrict the home page to only be available through a request to the Magento base URL.

Research

In order to complete the task we need to research the following high-level items:

1. How is the URL key for a CMS page specified?
2. How is a CMS page displayed when its URL key is requested?
3. How can we trigger the redirect?

Additional details such as accessing the current request path will be handled along the way.

The first step requires a look at the `cms/page` entity.
The second step requires working out how Magento processes requests, a process called *request flow*.
The third step requires looking for a suitable event - or a rewrite candidate - to inject our logic.

The cms/page Entity

Let's start with the easiest task. CMS pages are flat table entities, meaning they are stored in a single table - unlike EAV entities. The table name is `cms_page`.
An additional table called `cms_page_store` is used to keep the information for the store views in which a page is accessible - this second table can be ignored for this task though.

Looking at the `cms_page` table, two columns are the most interesting in regards to the request flow:

- The primary key column `page_id`
- The URL key column `identifier`

A CMS page can be accessed on the frontend if the request path matches the page's `identifier`. Before the identifier, the request path only contains the store base URL.

For example, if the configured Magento base URL is *http://magento.dev/shop/*, and the page's identifier is *enable-cookies*, then the full URL to view the CMS page would be *http://magento.dev/shop/enable-cookies*.

Let's dive in and have a look at how Magento figures that out internally.

Request Flow

Almost all of the request flow process we analyze in this section applies to all page requests, not just the ones related to CMS pages.

Each request starts with the *index.php* file in the Magento base directory.
In there, right at the end of the file, `Mage::run($mageRunCode, $mageRunType);` is called. We will look into how **$mageRunCode** and **$mageRunType** are used to to specify the store view in the chapter Store View Selection.
For now we will take a more generic view of the request flow process.

The call to `Mage::run()` does two things: first it causes the basic run time environment to be set up, and second it causes the request to be processed. That process is started by delegating to `Mage_Core_Model_App::run()`.
The following code block is an abbreviated version of that method and contains only the code most relevant for us:

```
public function run($params)
{
    // ... complete base setup ...
    if ($this->_cache->processRequest()) {
        $this->getResponse()->sendResponse();
    } else {
        // ... complete application initialization ...
        $this->getFrontController()->dispatch();
```

```
    }
    return $this;
}
```

Unless the cache processor is able to process the request, the Front Controller is initialized
and dispatched.

The cache processor is only relevant for the Enterprise Edition Full Page Cache module,
so we will not go into more detail about it here. Instead, let's have a look at the
Front Controller, which comes into play at the end of the code sample above when
`$this->getFrontController()` is called.

The Front Controller Routing Process

The Front Controller is the actual start of the routing process.[1]

This is what the getFrontController() method and the method _initFrontController()
it delegates to look like:

```
public function getFrontController()
{
    if (!$this->_frontController) {
        $this->_initFrontController();
    }

    return $this->_frontController;
}

protected function _initFrontController()
{
    $this->_frontController = new Mage_Core_Controller_Varien_Front();
    Mage::register('controller', $this->_frontController);
    $this->_frontController->init();
    return $this;
}
```

---

[1] When I first starting working with Magento, I thought the Front Controller would only be used for
requests to the Magento frontend - because of its name. This is not true. The Front Controller is called
Front Controller because it stands at the **front** of the routing process, before the routers and action
controllers take over. It actually is used for **all requests**.

On the first call to getFrontController(), the instance of
Mage_Core_Controller_Varien_Front is created. Then init() is called on it.
Let's look at that method first, before we continue with the dispatch() method after that.

```
/**
 * Init Front Controller
 *
 * @return Mage_Core_Controller_Varien_Front
 */
public function init()
{
    Mage::dispatchEvent('controller_front_init_before', array('front'=>$this));

    $routersInfo = Mage::app()->getStore()->getConfig(
        self::XML_STORE_ROUTERS_PATH
    );

    foreach ($routersInfo as $routerCode => $routerInfo) {
        if (isset($routerInfo['disabled']) && $routerInfo['disabled']) {
            continue;
        }
        if (isset($routerInfo['class'])) {
            $router = new $routerInfo['class'];
            if (isset($routerInfo['area'])) {
                $router->collectRoutes($routerInfo['area'], $routerCode);
            }
            $this->addRouter($routerCode, $router);
        }
    }

    Mage::dispatchEvent('controller_front_init_routers', array('front'=>$this));

    // Add default router at the last
    $default = new Mage_Core_Controller_Varien_Router_Default();
    $this->addRouter('default', $default);

    return $this;
}
```

What happens here is actually a very important part of the Magento routing logic.
All the Magento routers are initialized and added to the $this->_routers property of the

Front Controller.

This process is called *gathering all routers* (or *gathering all routes*, which is almost - but not *quite* - the same, as we will see below).

The question is, what is a router?

The purpose of a router is to analyze the browser request and check if it knows how to process it.

The actual processing of the request *may* then be handed off to an action controller (sometimes also called page controller).

To summarize what we have covered so far:

1. The Front Controller builds an array of router instances.
2. Each router checks if it can figure out what to do with a request.
3. The router that knows how to handle the request may then delegate to an action controller for processing.

The first routers are created and added to the **$_routers** array in the **foreach** loop in the previous code block.

The configuration section that the **foreach** iterates over can be found in the file *Mage/Core/etc/config.xml*[2]:

```
<default>
    <web>
        <routers>
            <admin>
                <area>admin</area>
                <class>Mage_Core_Controller_Varien_Router_Admin</class>
            </admin>
            <standard>
                <area>frontend</area>
                <class>Mage_Core_Controller_Varien_Router_Standard</class>
            </standard>
```

---

[2]Magento Trivia: the configuration section actually exists twice in that file: once under `stores/config/default` and once under `config/default`.

The former is only used if the current frontend store has the code `default`. If a different store is set as the current frontend store for the request, the latter config branch is used.

Technically it would have been enough to only specify the `config/default` value. When adding a custom router by adding to the configuration XML, it also needs to be specified in both sections.

Probably we will never know why both XML branches exist in the file.

```
        </routers>
    </web>
</default>
```

Each of those two routers are created in the **foreach** loop in the init() method.
After instantiation, collectRoutes(**$routerInfo**['area'], **$routerCode**) is called on each one, which causes it to create an array with the routes that are configured within the config XML branch specified by the **<area>** node.
More details on the route definition will be covered in the section The Route Configuration of the next chapter.

This is the *gather all routes* part mentioned earlier, as compared to gathering all *routers*. Put simply, routers contain a list of routes.

We will go into more detail later, but I think a bit of context regarding routes is required now. So here is a brief definition of a route.

A configured route is a mapping between a frontName and a module.
For example, **catalog** is the frontName provided by the **Mage_Catalog** module.

While building the list of mappings, each router doesn't only look in the specified config area, but also only will gather routes with a matching **<use>** node.

The standard router builds a list of all routes within the **<frontend>** config area containing a **<use>**standard**</use>** node.
The admin router builds a list of all routes within the **<admin>** area that contain a **<use>**admin**</use>** node.

We will look at the route configuration within the Create a Controller chapter in more detail.

Let's get back to the Front Controller (which still is building its list of routers where we left off to look at routes).

After the routers configured in the XML section are instantiated and added to the Front Controller's **$this->_routers** array, the event controller_front_init_routers is dispatched.

```
Mage::dispatchEvent('controller_front_init_routers', array('front'=>$this));
```

Looking for matching event observers, there will be one result within the Magento core, in *Mage/Cms/etc/config.xml*:[3]

---

[3]More on observer configuration later during the Event Observer section below.

```
<global>
    <events>
        <controller_front_init_routers>
            <observers>
                <cms>
                    <class>Mage_Cms_Controller_Router</class>
                    <method>initControllerRouters</method>
                </cms>
            </observers>
        </controller_front_init_routers>
    </events>
</global>
```

No observer model factory name is specified in the **<class>** node; instead, a regular PHP class name is used.

The observer method that is called on the class - **Mage_Cms_Controller_Router::initControllerRouters()** - is very simple:

```
public function initControllerRouters($observer)
{
    /* @var $front Mage_Core_Controller_Varien_Front */
    $front = $observer->getEvent()->getFront();

    $front->addRouter('cms', $this);
}
```

The **Mage_Cms** module's event observer adds itself to the list of routers of the Front Controller.

The question presents itself: why isn't the CMS router configured in the config XML, just like the **standard** and **admin** routers?

The only difference in the result is the order of the routers in the Front Controller's **$this->_routers** array

The routers configured in the config XML will be listed first, then the routers added via the event will be appended after them.

The following paragraph could almost be classified as Magento Trivia, but it actually is valuable to think it through. It serves to deepen the understanding of the config XML merge process, module dependencies, and how the Front Controller builds the routers array.

Because of module dependencies, the `Mage_Core` module will always be loaded before any other module. If the CMS router would have been configured using the XML method, the order of the routers would still be the same.

This is because the CMS modules section would be merged in to the config XML DOM structure after the `Mage_Core` module XML.

So there is no technical reason why the CMS router is added via an event observer.

How about a practical question: if we want to add a custom router to the Front Controller's array, is it better to use configuration XML or the `controller_front_init_routers` event?
The answer is (as usual): it depends.
If we want a custom router to be added *before* the CMS one, we should declare the router in the config XML.[4]
If we want the custom router to be added *after* the CMS router, the observer method has to be used.

Once we proceed to analyzing the Front Controller's `dispatch()` method, it will become clear why the sort order of the routers is important enough to spend so much time on it.

But first, let's finish dissecting the Front Controller's `init()` method - we are almost finished with it anyway.
The remaining code of the method adds one final router:

```
// Add default router at the last
$default = new Mage_Core_Controller_Varien_Router_Default();
$this->addRouter('default', $default);
```

Without resorting to hacks using PHP reflection, there is no way to add a custom router after it.
This `Default` router is used to display the configured 404 page if no other router knows how to handle a request[5]

To summarize, a Magento installation without any customizations uses 4 routers in the following order:

---

[4]We could also use the event observer approach, but in that case would also have to configure the `Mage_Cms` to depend on our extension, so our module's observer would be processed before the CMS one. Probably it is better to simply use the configuration XML instead.

[5]A name like `NoRoute` instead of `Default` would have been much more suitable for the final router.

Router	Class	Added via
admin	Mage_Core_Controller_Varien_Router_Admin	Config XML
standard	Mage_Core_Controller_Varien_Router_Standard	Config XML
cms	Mage_Cms_Controller_Router	Event Observer
default	Mage_Core_Controller_Varien_Router_Default	Hardcoded in Front Controller

Table 4.1: Magento Routers

Time to move on to the Front Controller's dispatch() method, where each router in turn is checked if it can match the current request.

```
public function dispatch()
{
    $request = $this->getRequest();

    // If pre-configured, check equality of base URL and requested URL
    $this->_checkBaseUrl($request);

    $request->setPathInfo()->setDispatched(false);
    if (!$request->isStraight()) {
        Mage::getModel('core/url_rewrite')->rewrite();
    }
    $this->rewrite();
    $i = 0;
    while (!$request->isDispatched() && $i++<100) {
        foreach ($this->_routers as $router) {
            if ($router->match($this->getRequest())) {
                break;
            }
        }
    }
    if ($i>100) {
        Mage::throwException(
            'Front controller reached 100 router match iterations'
        );
    }
    // This event gives possibility to launch something before sending
```

```
    // output (allow cookie setting)
    Mage::dispatchEvent(
        'controller_front_send_response_before', array('front'=>$this)
    );
    $this->getResponse()->sendResponse();
    Mage::dispatchEvent(
        'controller_front_send_response_after', array('front'=>$this)
    );
    return $this;
}
```

The matching of the routers happens in the **foreach** loop within in the **while** near the center of the method.
This nested set of loops requires some explanation.

Before we dive in further: the counter variable **$i** is just a sentry flag to avoid Magento getting stuck in an infinite loop. Unless you encounter a bug, it will never hit a count higher than 2.

The main indicator for the outer loop to exit is the isDispatched flag on the request object.
As long as the isDispatched flag is **false**, it will continue.

The inner **foreach** loop iterates over all routers added during init().
The match() method is called on each of the routers in turn.

The purpose of the match() method is to check if a router knows how to *process the request.* *Processing the request* means generating the response that will be sent back to the browser.

The response may consist of a full response body, or may only contain HTTP headers (for example in case of a redirect). Either case qualifies as the request being processed.

If a response was generated, the router's match() method will set the isDispatched flag on the request to **true**, and the outer loop will exit.

Besides processing the request and generating output, a router also has another option: it can modify the **$request** object without setting the isDispatched flag to **true**.

In that case the outer loop will continue, and a different router may now process the request, since it has been modified.
This is how one router delegates to a another.

The following table shows the different cases that might occur while the nested loop is being processed, depending on the value returned by the match() method and the isDispatched flag.

match()	isDispatched	Request modified	Response generated	Continue with
false	false	no	no	Continue inner loop
true	false	yes	no	Exit inner loop, continue outer loop
true	true	doesn't matter	yes	Exit both loops

Table 4.2: Front Controller routing

To fully understand this process, it is important to know that the final router - the Default 404 page router - always matches.
It takes advantage of the option to delegate to a different router.

The Default router always modifies the request to point to the configured 404 page and returns **true** as the result of the match() method, while keeping isDispatched set to **false**.

The result is that the process breaks out of the inner loop, but the outer loop continues, and so the inner iteration over the routers begins again.
However, this time the Standard router is able to match the modified request, so it will generate the response (the 404 page content) and set the isDispatched flag to **true**.

The following list of steps taken might help to illustrate when a non-existent route is accessed:

1. The outer loop starts (isDispatched is **false**)
2. The Admin router's match() returns **false**
3. The Standard router's match() returns **false**
4. The CMS router's match() returns **false**
5. The Default router match() method is called

   1. It modifies the request object
   2. It returns **true** (but isDispatched still is false)

6. The inner loop exits (because match() returned **true**)
7. The outer loop continues (because isDispatched still is **false**)
8. The inner loop starts again
9. The Admin router still doesn't match

10. The Standard router's `match()` method is called again

   1. It recognizes the values on the modified request object
   2. It processes the request (that is, it generates output)
   3. It sets `isDispatched` to **true**
   4. It returns **true**

11. The inner loop exits (because `match()` returned **true**)
12. The outer loop exits (because `isDispatched` is **true**).

The following table describes the requests each router matches and how the match is handled.

#	Router	Matches	Match type
1	Admin	Routes configured in the `<admin>` area	Generate content
2	Standard	Routes configured in the `<frontend>` area	Generate content
3	CMS	Requests matching a CMS Page identifier	Delegate to **Standard** router
4	Default	Always matches (404 page)	Delegate to **Standard** router

Table 4.3: Router matching overview

In terms of this chapter's exercise, this information is relevant: the match type of the CMS router.
According to the table, the CMS router `Mage_Cms_Controller_Router` also delegates to the Standard router to display the page content (just like the Default router).
This means that we can focus on the functioning of the Standard router in order to understand how the CMS page output is generated.

Also, the Admin router extends the Standard router class, thereby inheriting the `Mage_Core_Controller_Varien_Router_Standard::match()` method.

To summarize: in a native Magento installation, every page request always ends up being processed by the Standard router's `match()` method.
This happens either through a direct match, through class inheritance, or through delegation from anther router.

Before we examine how the Standard router's `match()` method works, let's see how exactly the delegation from one router to another happens.

We will use the CMS router as an example.
The following code block is an excerpt from the `Mage_Cms_Controller_Router::match()` method.

```
$identifier = trim($request->getPathInfo(), '/');

$page    = Mage::getModel('cms/page');
$pageId = $page->checkIdentifier(
    $identifier, Mage::app()->getStore()->getId()
);
if (!$pageId) {
    return false;
}

$request->setModuleName('cms')
    ->setControllerName('page')
    ->setActionName('view')
    ->setParam('page_id', $pageId);

return true;
```

In short, if a CMS page with an identifier matching the current request path info is found, the request is modified to delegate to the `Standard` router.

This is what the call to `setModuleName()`, `setControllerName()` and `setActionName()` is all about.

The delegation from `Default` to the `Standard` router in order to display the configured 404 page is done in exactly the same way.

The Standard Router

Now it is time to have a look at how the
`Mage_Core_Controller_Varien_Router_Standard::match()` process works.
The method is quite long, so here we will break it up into several different parts. Each part will still be an abbreviated version of the core code to make it easier to follow.

```
public function match(Zend_Controller_Request_Http $request)
{
```

```
$front = $this->getFront();
$path = trim($request->getPathInfo(), '/');

if ($path) {
    $p = explode('/', $path);
} else {
    $p = explode('/', $this->_getDefaultPath());
}
```

The variable **$p** is set to contain the request path split at the / character.

If the request path is empty, the return value of _getDefaultPath() is used. This value is taken from the system configuration option found at *Web > Default Pages > Default Web URL*, which defaults to simply 'cms'.

Because of this, for a request to the base URL of a Magento instance, **$p** will look as follows:

```
Array
(
    [0] => cms
)
```

For a request to */customer/account/login*, **$p** would be:

```
Array
(
    [0] => customer
    [1] => account
    [2] => login
)
```

Of course there might be more parts to the request path, which would lead to more records in the array.

The next part of the match() method processes the first part of the array.

```
// get module name
if ($request->getModuleName()) {
    $module = $request->getModuleName();
```

```
    } else {
        if (!empty($p[0])) {
            $module = $p[0];
        } else {
            $module = $this->getFront()->getDefault('module');
        }
    }

    $modules = $this->getModuleByFrontName($module);

    if ($modules === false) {
        return false;
    }
```

The variable $module is set to the first part of the request.

However, if $request->getModuleName() returns something, it will take precedence over the first entry in $p. This will be the case if a previous router has set the module name in order to delegate to the Standard router.

In the rare case[6] that neither getModuleName() returns a value nor $p[0] is set, the default module is fetched from the Front Controller (setting $module to the value 'core').[7]

Whatever the details, the important thing to remember is: the first part of the request path is set to $module.

The value of $module is used as the frontName for the request.

The frontName points to one or more modules which might have controllers that can process the current request. This mapping from the frontName to a list of modules is done in the config XML.

The router gets the list of modules via the method getModuleByFrontName().

The exact syntax for configuring this mapping of frontNames to modules in config XML will be covered later in the Create a Controller and Controller Rewrite chapters.

If $module doesn't match a configured frontName, the match() method returns false, that is, the Standard router can not come up with a match (see the last paragraph of the previous code block above).

---

[6]That could only happen if the default page configuration web/default/front is set to an empty string.

[7]Magento Trivia: The default values are set on the Front Controller by the router in the beginning of the match() method while fetchDefault() is called. Later that value is read back again from the Front Controller into the router. This was omitted from the code in the book because it is somewhat confusing (and unimportant); please inspect the real source code to see yourself.
Does this make sense? I don't think I'm smart enough to judge...

However, if at least one possible module is mapped to the `frontName`, the matching process continues as follows.

```
/**
 * Going through modules to find appropriate controller
 */
$found = false;
foreach ($modules as $realModule) {
    if ($request->getControllerName()) {
        $controller = $request->getControllerName();
    } else {
        if (!empty($p[1])) {
            $controller = $p[1];
        } else {
            $controller = $front->getDefault('controller');
        }
    }
}
```

The router iterates over the possible modules, and looks for a controller class matching the second part of the request (`$p[1]`).

Each iteration tries to match the request to a controller in a different module. The module being checked is stored in the variable `$realModule` by the `foreach` statement.

For example, let's assume the front name `catalog` is mapped to the modules `Mage_Catalog` and `Example_Module_Catalog` using config XML.
For a request to *http://magento.dev/catalog*, during the iteration those two values would be assigned in turn to `$realModule`.

To clarify:

Variable	Contents	Example
`$module`	The request `frontName`.	catalog
`$modules`	The modules mapped to the `frontName`	Array('Mage_Catalog', 'Example_Module_Catalog')
`$realModule`	A concrete module from `$modules` being checked for a matching controller.	Mage_Catalog

Table 4.4: Values used during the request matching

Luckily the value of `$realModule` is not used a lot during module development.
It usually is only used during the `Standard` router matching process.

Inside the `foreach` loop, the `$controller` variable is set to the second part of the request pat.
Similar to the setting of `$module`, if `$request->getControllerName()` returns a string, it takes priority over `$p[1]`.
Again, this will be the case if a previous router set the value to delegate to the `Standard` router.

In case neither `getControllerName()` returns a value nor `$p[1]` is set, the default controller name is fetched from the Front Controller.
This will set `$controller` to `'index'`.

Please refer to the code block above to see the code discussed so far.

Now that `$realModule` and `$controller` are set, let's move on.

```
// get action name
if ($request->getActionName()) {
    $action = $request->getActionName();
} else {
    $action = !empty($p[2]) ? $p[2] : $front->getDefault('action');
}
```

The third part of the request path is assigned to the variable `$action`, unless `$request->getActionName()` was set by a previous router's `match()` method.

The default value for the action name is `index`, just like for `$controller`.[8]

```
$controllerClassName = $this
    ->_validateControllerClassName($realModule, $controller);
if (!$controllerClassName) {
    continue;
}
```

Now that `$realModule, $controller` and `$action` are set, the router finally checks if a matching controller file really exists.

---

[8]Magento Trivia: In case you wondered why the determination of the values for `$controller` and `$action` happens inside the loop, even though they will always be the same on each iteration: yes indeed, that once again isn't the best implementation. Luckily, the list of modules for a `frontName` never is very long.

In order to map the second part of the request **$controller** to a file, the standard router follows this process:

1. Replace all _ in **$realModule** with /
2. Uppercase the first character of each word
3. Prefix the full path to the **$realModule**'s *controllers* directory.
4. Append **$controller**
5. Append *Controller.php* to the file name

Since a bit of code might be easier to understand, here is the method in question:

```
public function getControllerFileName($realModule, $controller)
{
    $parts = explode('_', $realModule);
    $realModule = implode('_', array_splice($parts, 0, 2));
    $file = Mage::getModuleDir('controllers', $realModule);
    if (count($parts)) {
        $file .= DS . implode(DS, $parts);
    }
    $file .= DS.uc_words($controller, DS).'Controller.php';
    return $file;
}
```

For example, given **$realModule** is set to Mage_Catalog and **$controller** is set to product, the controller class would be Mage_Catalog_ProductController.

For security reasons, the routing process follows a very strict set of rules when mapping the request path (which is user input) to a file. That is why every controller class has the Controller suffix.

That is also why the full file system path is built, and the PHP include path is not used to find controller class files.

The Standard router uses the **$realModule** value to determine the full path to the module directory, and then adds a lower case *controllers* directory to it. This is to break the Magento autoloader.

Once again, security. I guess it is better to be paranoid than sorry.

To continue the example, the controller file for the class Mage_Catalog_ProductController would be .../app/code/core/Mage/Catalog/controllers/ProductController.php.

Note that the *controllers* directory is added after the **first 2** parts of the controller class name!
Here are some examples:

$realModule value	controllers directory
Mage_Catalog	*Mage/Catalog/controllers*
Meeting02_Example	*Meeting02/Example/controllers*
Mage_Widget_Adminhtml	*Mage/Widget/controllers/Adminhtml*
Example_Module_Catalog	*Example/Module/controllers/Catalog*

Table 4.5: Examples for $realModule values mapped to module *controllers* directories

If the resulting controller file does not exist, the Standard router will continue to look for the file in the next module mapped to by the frontName.

However, if the controller file exists, it will be included, and the controller class is instantiated as can be seen in the following code block
(just as a quick reminder: we are still discussing the match() method of the Standard router).

```
    // instantiate controller class
    $controllerInstance = Mage::getControllerInstance(
        $controllerClassName, $request, $front->getResponse()
    );

    if (!$controllerInstance->hasAction($action)) {
        continue;
    }

    $found = true;
    break;
}

if (!$found) {
    return false;
}
```

Finally, the router checks if a matching action method exists on the controller.

The name of the PHP method to call for a given action is determined by adding the suffix `Action` to the variable `$action`.

For example, the action `index` is handled by a method `indexAction()` of the controller.

In case no matching action is found, the `Standard` router will continue looking in the next module mapped to by the `frontName`.

If all `$modules` were checked without finding a matching controller with a matching action, `false` is returned.

In this case the `Standard` router was not able to match the current request, and the Front Controller will continue with the next router.

On the other hand, if a match was found, there are a number of final steps before the controller's action method is called.

```
// set values only after all the checks are done
$request->setModuleName($module);
$request->setControllerName($controller);
$request->setActionName($action);
$request->setControllerModule($realModule);

// dispatch action
$request->setDispatched(true);
$controllerInstance->dispatch($action);

return true;
}
```

The `frontName`, controller, action and the `$realModule` are set on the request object. This can be very handy if, for example, we need to find out what page is currently being requested inside an event observer.

Then the `isDispatched` flag is set to `true` (finally!), and the router delegates to the controller by calling `dispatch()`.

Finally we have completed reading through the `Standard` routers `match()` method!

Standard Router Summary

Before we continue analyzing the request processing inside the action controller, let's summarize the routing process from the `Standard` router context.

The steps the `Standard` router's `match()` method takes are:

1. Split the request path into parts (using /)
2. Match the first part to a module directory (using XML configuration)
3. Match the second part to a controller file (by file name)
4. Match the third part to an action method (by method name)
5. If a matching controller class was found, `dispatch()` is called on it

For some developers it is confusing that the `frontName` is mapped to a module directory using configuration XML.
The request `frontName` can be completely different than the module's directory name, as will become apparent in the following two chapters.

However, when mapping the controller to a controller class there is a direct correlation between the controller name and the file system.

As stated once before, the action method name is found by appending an *Action* suffix to the third part of the request path.
If no controller or action were specified in the request, the default controller and action values are used, which both are `index` (mapping to an *IndexController.php* file or an `indexAction()` method respectively).

If a matching controller is found, the response content is generated by dispatching the action controller. Note that all this happens while the router's `match()` is called.
Maybe a better name for the method would have been `matchAndProcess()`.

The Front Controller Responsibilities

Because knowing the workings of the Front Controller is useful beyond passing the MCD exam, there is more to be said about it.

So far we only have discussed the aspects of the Front Controller directly related to the routing process, that is, the gathering of all routes and finding a matching router.

There are 3 further responsibilities:

- Applying database based URL rewrites
- Applying config XML based regular expression URL rewrites
- Sending the response

All of these are handled inside the Front Controller's `dispatch()` method. In addition to these three, there are a few additional aspects - like additional events - that are quite useful to know about.

Let's look at these in order to complete our understanding of the Front Controller.

Applying database based URL rewrites

```
if (!$request->isStraight()) {
    Mage::getModel('core/url_rewrite')->rewrite();
}
```

This code segment is found at the beginning of the `dispatch()` method.
Unless the `isStraight` flag is set on the request, database based rewrites are applied first.[9]

The DB based rewrites are stored in in the table `core_url_rewrite`.

If the current request path matches the `request_path` field for the current store, the request object will be modified and further processing will take place as if the `target_path` column value was the requested path instead.

The catalog SEO friendly URLs are implemented using this rewrite mechanism.

The catalog-related records in `core_url_rewrite` are created by the URL indexer.

It is also possible to add custom URL rewrite records using the adminhtml backend. Many projects also add rewrites using custom PHP scripts, too.

One thing to watch out for is that the table doesn't grow too large over time. There is no real safeguard for that available in Magento.

It is useful to have a look at the real table. You will probably find it is rather straightforward.

Applying config XML based regular expression URL rewrites

```
$this->rewrite();
```

Not a lot of code. It has changed a little in newer Magento versions since 1.7.0.2 on which, as a reminder, the current version of the certification is currently based.

---

[9]The `isStraight` flag is only set on the request object by the Enterprise Edition Full Page Cache module under certain conditions, so we will not explore that any further here.

The main purpose is still the same though.
The configuration based requests rewrites are applied right after the previous, DB based ones.

This type of URL rewrites has been declared deprecated, but is still available for backward compatibility. It sets the requests path info on the request object to the matched value.

An example configuration to rewrite all requests to */customer/account/loginPost* to a custom controller action would look as follows:

```
<global>
    <rewrite>
        <example_rewrite>
            <from>#^/customer/account/loginPost(.*)$#i</from>
            <to>/example/login/post$1</to>
            <!--<complete>1</complete>-->
        </example_rewrite>
    </rewrite>
</global>
```

The **$_rewritedPathInfo** property on the request object will be set to the original path info that was requested, unless the **<complete>** node is set in the configuration.

If **$_rewritedPathInfo** is set (because **<complete>** is missing), URLs using the wildcard * character to refer to the current module, current controller, or current action will be constructed using the original request path.

Kind of confusing, and the naming choice of the node doesn't help.
What it boils down to is that that the original path info will be used to construct new URLs if **<complete>** is set. The name **<use_orig_pathinfo>** would have been much more descriptive.

An example for a URL being constructed using wildcards would be
Mage::getUrl('*/*/list') (current frontName, current controller, list action).

Generally it is better to omit the **<complete>** tag, since complete regex based URL rewrites can lead to having to rewrite further controllers or actions than wanted because of that behavior.

Assuming the XML rewrite example above from */customer/account/loginPost* to */example/login/post* is in effect, Mage::getUrl('*/*/test') would return the following request path:

Request path before rewrite	Configuration	Request path after rewrite
/customer/account/loginPost	Without `<complete>`	*/customer/account/test*
/customer/account/loginPost	With `<complete>`	*/example/login/test*

Table 4.6: `Mage::getUrl('*/*/test')` results differences with or without `<complete>`

The first version probably gives the desired result, unless you really are planning to rewrite further requests to */customer/account/* to the same custom controller.

Sending the response

```
// This event gives possibility to launch something before sending
// output (allow cookie setting)
Mage::dispatchEvent('
    controller_front_send_response_before', array('front'=>$this)
);
$this->getResponse()->sendResponse();
Mage::dispatchEvent('
    controller_front_send_response_after', array('front'=>$this)
);
```

The fifth and final Front Controller responsibility - displayed in the code block above - is also part of the `dispatch()` method.

After the routing has taken place and the response has been generated, it is the final responsibility of the Front Controller to flush it to the browser.

This is the reason why no output should be echoed out directly from a controller action (or anywhere).

If some content is printed directly, bypassing the Front Controller, it would no longer be possible to add HTTP headers to the response after the routing completes.

Also, it would be impossible to capture and process the content that already was sent using the handy `controller_front_send_response_before` event you can see being dispatched in the code snippet above.

Instead, any response data should always be added to the response object using `$response->setBody()`, `$response->appendBody()` or `$response->setHeader()`.

That way the response content may be modified or new headers may be added via event observers right up to the the moment the Front Controller calls `$this->getResponse()->sendResponse()`.

Many caching modules for Magento rely on content being set on the response object, including the Enterprise Edition Full Page Cache.

Secondary Responsibility: Check the base URL

```
// If pre-configured, check equality of base URL and requested URL
$this->_checkBaseUrl($request);
```

There is one additional task the Front Controller takes care of at the beginning of the `dispatch()` method, and that is to check that the requested URL matches the configured base URL for the current store.

The line of code was omitted from the larger code sections of the `dispatch()` method further above in order to focus on the routing logic.

The purpose of the method `_checkBaseUrl()` is to redirect a visitor to the configured base URL if the current request doesn't match it.

For example, let's assume that the webserver is configured to serve Magento on both the *www.example.com* and *example.com* domains.

Without the base URL check, that would mean every page is available on two different domains. Google would rate that as duplicate content, and reduce both sites' rank.

For that reason, if the base URL configured in the system configuration is set to, let's say, *http://www.example.com/*, then requests to *http://example.com/* are automatically redirected to the version of the domain with the *www* prefix.

That way there is only a single resource on the web with the content, and thus Google no longer sees it as duplicate content.

Please note that it is a smarter approach to configure redirects to a single base URL on the webserver instead of in Magento, since that causes much less overhead.
For the Apache webserver `mod_rewrite` offers the option to add rewrite rules. Other webservers have similar capabilities that can be used to the same effect.

The base URL check in Magento can be disabled in the system configuration with the option `web/url/redirect_to_base`.

Checking the base URL is not considered one of the prime responsibilities of the Front Controller, but it still is useful to know about it.

Summary of the Front Controller responsibilities:

The Front Controller has 5 main responsibilities:

1. Gathering all routes
2. DB based request rewrites
3. Config XML based (regex) request rewrites
4. Finding a matching router
5. Sending output

The purpose of a router is to provide a way to match requests to specific business logic.

An example from a real project for a custom router was a site where requests where mapped to articles by date, author or keywords, or combinations thereof.
The standard router matching doesn't fit that scheme at all, so a custom router was an elegant solution.

However, usually the actual request processing and the generation of the response content is not done by the router class itself.
That task is delegated to an action controller.

For that reason, most core routers simply modify the response object[10] without setting the `isDispatched` flag, so the `Standard` router will match the request on the next iteration.

The Action Controller Dispatch Process

Once the `Standard` router has matched a request and found a matching action controller, it will call `dispatch()` on it, passing along the requested action name.

---

[10]More specific, they set the module, controller and action name on the request object to delegate to the `Standard` router.

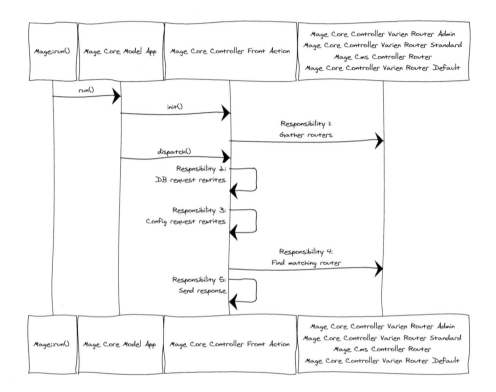

Figure 4.1. The Front Controller Responsibilities

```
// dispatch action
$request->setDispatched(true);
$controllerInstance->dispatch($action);
```

All controllers inherit the `dispatch()` method from the abstract class `Mage_Core_Controller_Varien_Action`.

The following code block is very abbreviated. The purpose is to illustrate the structure of the `dispatch()` method:

```
public function dispatch($actionMethodName)
{
    $this->preDispatch();

    if ($this->getRequest()->isDispatched()) {
        if (!$this->getFlag('', self::FLAG_NO_DISPATCH)) {
            $this->$actionMethodName();
            $this->postDispatch();
        }
    }
}
```

Remember, when this method is called by the Front Controller, the request `isDispatched` flag has already been set to **true**.

The structure of the `dispatch()` method offers two options that can be taken advantage of in the `preDispatch()` method:

- If the `isDispatched` flag is reverted to **false**, the controller action will not be processed after all.
  This opens the possibility to delegate to a different router from an action controller, since the outer router matching loop of the Front Controller will continue after the match.
- If the `Mage_Core_Controller_Varien_Action::FLAG_NO_DISPATCH` flag is set on the action controller, the action method will not be called.
  The difference to the previous option is that in this case no further router matching will take place, since `isDispatched` still is **true**.
  This allows the complete response to be generated during the `preDispatch()` method.

Let's inspect the (abbreviated) `preDispatch()` method code to see how this might be utilized.

```
public function preDispatch()
{
    if ($this->_rewrite()) {
        return;
    }

    if (!$this->getFlag('', self::FLAG_NO_START_SESSION)) {
        $session = Mage::getSingleton(
            'core/session', array('name' => $this->_sessionNamespace)
        )->start();
    }

    Mage::app()->loadArea($this->getLayout()->getArea());

    Mage::dispatchEvent(
        'controller_action_predispatch',
        array('controller_action' => $this)
    );
    Mage::dispatchEvent(
        'controller_action_predispatch_' . $this->getRequest()->getRouteName(),
        array('controller_action' => $this)
    );
    Mage::dispatchEvent(
        'controller_action_predispatch_' . $this->getFullActionName(),
        array('controller_action' => $this)
    );
}
```

First, right at the top of the method, another round of rewrites is applied. We will delve into this _rewrite() method later on.

Second, the session is started, unless the FLAG_NO_START_SESSION flag is set on the action controller.
This flag might come in handy when writing integration tests and you don't feel like mocking the session model.
However, the most important thing to remember is that the session is started by the action controller's preDispatch() method.

Then the current request area is loaded on the core/app model.
More on area loading later while discussing event observer configuration.

Third, 3 events are dispatched. They range from very generic to very specific.

- The `controller_action_predispatch` event is dispatched for every page request in Magento.
- The `controller_action_predispatch_` event with the name of the current route appended is dispatched next.
  The `Standard` router sets the route name on the request object using
  `$request->setRouteName($this->getRouteByFrontName($module))`.
  We will have a closer look at route names in the following chapter Create a Controller. This event is much more specific then the previous one, but still is the same for every page request within one route configuration.
- The final event is `controller_action_predispatch_`, followed by the full action name.
  The full action name consists of three parts:

    1. The route name
    2. The controller name
    3. The action name

Usually these three parts are concatenated using an underscore. This results in an event name specific to every page in Magento.

For example, a request to the URL path *`/catalog/product/view`* would cause the following three events to be dispatched from the action controller's `preDispatch()` method:

1. `controller_action_predispatch`
2. `controller_action_predispatch_catalog`
3. `controller_action_predispatch_catalog_product_view`

The third one of these events is by far the most useful.

In fact, this finally brings us back to our main exercise objective:
redirect visitors back to the base URL if the configured home page is requested directly by its page identifier.

This event is used in the exercise solution code to check if the current request is for the configured home page.

But let's not get ahead of ourselves, as there is one more thing to discuss before moving on to the solution.

Setting Flags on action controllers

```
public function setFlag($action, $flag, $value)
{
    if (''===$action) {
        $action = $this->getRequest()->getActionName();
    }
    $this->_flags[$action][$flag] = $value;
    return $this;
}

public function getFlag($action, $flag='')
{
    if (''===$action) {
        $action = $this->getRequest()->getActionName();
    }
    if (''===$flag) {
        return $this->_flags;
    }
    elseif (isset($this->_flags[$action][$flag])) {
        return $this->_flags[$action][$flag];
    }
    else {
        return false;
    }
}
```

Controller flags are key-value pairs.

Each flag is set for a specific action. Usually an empty string is used as the action name, which means it will simply be set for the current action.

The core uses a number of flags to switch some behavior of the action controller on or off, like the FLAG_NO_DISPATCH or FLAG_NO_START_SESSION we have discussed earlier. These flag names are available as class constants in the abstract class Mage_Core_Controller_Varien_Action.

Besides using flags as switches, they can also be used to store any key-value pairs on controllers, kind of like setData() can be used on Varien_Object instances.

Here is an example of a flag being set on the action to prohibit the session from being started:

```
$action = Mage::app()->getFrontController()->getAction();
$action->setFlag(
    '', Mage_Core_Controller_Varien_Action::FLAG_NO_START_SESSION, 1
);
```

The following code block is an example to set and get custom values on an action controller

```
// get the action controller
$action = Mage::app()->getFrontController()->getAction();

// set custom flag
$action->setFlag('', 'request-cache-id', 'AB19534TG6');

// get custom flag value
$action->getFlag('', 'request-cache-id');
```

Action Controller Request Rewrites

Close to the beginning of the `preDispatch()` method, another set of configuration based rewrites are applied to the request.
The method that is called to do this is
`Mage_Core_Controller_Varien_Action::_rewrite()`.

However, this type of configuration based rewrite has also been declared deprecated, just like the Front Controller configuration based rewrites.
The reason for that is that the whole overhead of routing that has happened up to this point is wasted if a rewrite is configured using this method.

Similar to the regular expression config based request rewrites applied by the Front Controller, this rewrite facility still exists solely for backward compatibility.

You might encounter it in third party extensions, so it is a good thing to know about it.

The config based rewrite configuration that is applied by the action controller comes in two flavors:

1. Rewrite all actions of a given controller
2. Rewrite only specific actions.

For example, rewriting all requests to the `checkout/cart` controller to a custom `example/special_cart` controller would look like this:

```
<!-- global only (not frontend or adminhtml) -->
<global>
    <routers>
        <!-- route name -->
        <checkout>
            <rewrite>
                <!-- controller name -->
                <cart>
                    <!-- rewrite all controller actions -->
                    <override_actions>false</override_actions>
                    <to>example/special_cart</to>
                </cart>
            </rewrite>
        </checkout>
    </routers>
</global>
```

To only rewrite a specific action, the **<override_actions>** node is omitted and the action is added as a child node.

For example, to only rewrite the add action of the checkout/cart controller, the following code would be used:

```
<!-- global only (not frontend or admin) -->
<global>
    <routers>
        <!-- route name -->
        <checkout>
            <rewrite>
                <!-- controller name -->
                <cart>
                    <actions>
                        <!-- action name -->
                        <add>
                            <to>example/special_cart/add</to>
                        </add>
                    </actions>
                </cart>
            </rewrite>
        </checkout>
    </routers>
</global>
```

Regardless whether the route which is being rewritten is configured in the `frontend` or `admin` area, the rewrite always is specified in the `<global>` branch.

Wrap-Up Summary of the Exercise Research

We started this section defining three things we need to know in order to implement the exercise solution:

1. How is the URL key for a CMS page specified?
2. How is a CMS page displayed when its URL key is requested?
3. How can we trigger the redirect?

It was a long section, so let's summarize the findings.

How is the URL key for a CMS page specified?

This has a straightforward answer: the CMS page URL key is specified using the `cms/page` attribute `identifier`.

How is a CMS page displayed when its URL key is requested?

1. `Mage_Core_Model_App::run()` initializes the Front Controller and calls its `dispatch()` method.
2. The Front Controller gathers a list of all routers and proceeds to find one matching the current request.
3. The CMS router checks if the request path matches a CMS page identifier and modifies the request object to delegate to the `Standard` router if that is the case.
4. The `Standard` router now can match the modified request, and it delegates to the action controller `Mage_Cms_PageController::viewAction()` method for processing.

How can we trigger the redirect?

Before the actual action method is called, the controller's `preDispatch()` method dispatches the page specific event `controller_action_predispatch_cms_page_view`.

Our redirect can be implemented in an event observer for this event.

The redirect itself is set on the response object instead of calling the PHP function `header()` directly, because the sending of the response is handled by the Front Controller.

To prohibit further processing of the request, the `Mage_Core_Controller_Varien_Action::FLAG_NO_DISPATCH` controller flag is set on the action controller instance.

Solution

The code can be found in the extension `Meeting02_RedirectToRoot`.
After a long research section, the solution code is very short.

An event observer for the event `controller_action_predispatch_cms_page_view` is declared in the configuration XML.

```
<frontend>
    <events>
        <controller_action_predispatch_cms_page_view>
            <observers>
                <meeting02_redirectToRoot>
                    <type>model</type>
                    <class>meeting02_redirectToRoot/observer</class>
                    <method>controllerActionPredispatchCmsPageView</method>
                </meeting02_redirectToRoot>
            </observers>
        </controller_action_predispatch_cms_page_view>
    </events>
</frontend>
```

Event Dispatch Process and Observer Configuration

Event observers are one of the most powerful tools of a Magento developer.
Even though the implementation in Magento isn't perfect, it is still possible to use them to great effect.
However, once again it is useful to have a good understanding of how they work.

Let's analyze the event system code, starting with the method call which triggers an event:

```
Mage::dispatchEvent($eventCode, $eventArguments);
```

The event code is a string. If the optional **$eventArguments** argument is present it must be an array of key-value pairs which will be passed to the observer method as arguments, as we will see shortly.

As often is the case, the `Mage` "god" class uses a delegate to do the real work.

```
public static function dispatchEvent($name, array $data = array())
{
    $result = self::app()->dispatchEvent($name, $data);
    return $result;
}
```

In this case `Mage` delegates to the application model `Mage_Core_Model_App`, where the main event dispatching process takes place.

Let's dissect the `Mage_Core_Model_App::dispatchEvent()` method bit by bit.

```
public function dispatchEvent($eventName, $args)
{
    foreach ($this->_events as $area=>$events) {
```

The first thing that happens is that Magento iterates over an array containing the registered event areas.
So what are these?

Event Areas

When the `core/app` model is instantiated, the **$_events** property is an empty array.

Then, when the Magento application initialization is triggered by calling `Mage::run()` or `Mage::app()`, the global events area is registered.
This happens by calling

```
Mage::app()->loadAreaPart(
    Mage_Core_Model_App_Area::AREA_GLOBAL,
    Mage_Core_Model_App_Area::PART_EVENTS
);
```

You can find this code in `Mage::app()` and `Mage_Core_Model_App::run()`.

The end effect is that a record is added to the `core/app::$_events` property with the area name as the key.
The value is - once again - an empty array.

```
$this->_events = array('global' => array())
```

Once an event area is "loaded" in this way, the **foreach** loop in `core/app::dispatchEvent()` will process the configuration within that config XML branch matching that area (please refer to the loop in the code block a little further above).

The `loadAreaPart()` only registers the area in the array. The actual configuration is lazy-loaded whenever an event is dispatched.

Instead of using `loadAreaPart()`, the method `Mage::app()->addEventArea($area);` can be called alternatively.
The end result is the same.

This alternative `addEventArea()` method is used in the *cron.php* script to register the `crontab` event area.

In addition to the `global` event area, the `frontend` or `adminhtml` event areas are loaded during the action controller's `preDispatch()` method, depending on whether it is a frontend or admin controller.

The following table gives an overview over where the different event areas are loaded.

Event Area	Loaded in
global	`Mage::app()`
	`Mage::run()`
frontend	`Mage_Core_Controller_Front_Action::preDispatch()`
adminhtml	`Mage_Adminhtml_Controller_Action::preDispatch()`
	`Mage_Api_Model_Server_Handler_Abstract::_construct()`
crontab	*cron.php* file

Table 4.7: Event Areas

Before the action controller is dispatched, only events configured under the **<global>** config XML area will be processed.

This is good to know, especially when registering an event observer for the early events dispatched by the Front Controller.
Putting them in **<frontend>** or **<adminhtml>** just won't work.

When writing custom command line scripts which initialize the Magento environment, keep in mind that no area besides **global** is registered when calling **Mage::app()**.

Even setting a store view by calling **Mage::app()->setCurrentStore($storeCode)** doesn't magically load the events for that store's area.

If you want the **adminhtml** or **frontend** events to be processed, the event area needs to be loaded manually as shown in the following example code block.

```
require_once 'app/Mage.php';
Mage::app('admin');
Mage::app()->addEventArea('adminhtml');
```

Getting back on track dissecting the **core/app::dispatchEvent()** method...
When an event is dispatched, and no configuration for that event was previously loaded for a registered area, the event configuration is loaded via the config model:

```
if (!isset($events[$eventName])) {
    $eventConfig = $this->getConfig()->getEventConfig($area, $eventName);
    if (!$eventConfig) {
        $this->_events[$area][$eventName] = false;
        continue;
    }
}
```

The **$eventConfig** variable will contain the full **config/[area]/events/[event-name]** branch from the config XML.
Next, this configuration is processed to find all observers that are registered for the current event.

```
$observers = array();
foreach ($eventConfig->observers->children() as $obsName=>$obsConfig) {
    $observers[$obsName] = array(
        'type'  => (string)$obsConfig->type,
        'model' => $obsConfig->class ?
```

```
                        (string)$obsConfig->class :
                        $obsConfig->getClassName(),
                  'method'=> (string)$obsConfig->method,
                  'args'  => (array)$obsConfig->args,
            );
      }
      $events[$eventName]['observers'] = $observers;
      $this->_events[$area][$eventName]['observers'] = $observers;
   }
```

The configuration is processed and the result is assigned to the
`Mage_Core_Model_App::$_events[$area][$eventName]` array.

We can see the code checks for the following nodes

- `<type>`
- `<class>` or `<model>`[11]
- `<method>`
- `<args>`[12]

All of these nodes must be wrapped by a unique node, called observer name (assigned to
the variable `$obsName` by the foreach statement).

The only purpose of the observer name is to avoid conflicts between modules that register
observers for the same events.
That's why it is important to use a unique node as the observer name.

According to best practice, use namespace - underscore - module name in lower case. This
follows the same convention as the class group for a module.

Here is an example observer configuration:

```
<config>
    <frontend>
        <events>
            <customer_login>
                <observers>
```

---

[11]As mentioned before, nobody uses `<model>` (even though it works), so it probably is a good idea to
stick to the convention and use `<class>`.

[12]Nothing is done with the value of the `<args>` node in the event observer configuration - it is completely
ignored after it is read.

```
                            <example_module>
                                <type>singleton</type>
                                <class>example_module/observer</class>
                                <method>customerLogin</method>
                            </example_module>
                        </observers>
                    </customer_login>
                </events>
            </frontend>
</config>
```

Node	Value	Comment
Event Name	customer_login	Code passed to Mage::dispatchEvent()
Observer Name	example_module	Unique node ([namespace]_[module])
\<type\>	singleton	Instantiation type
\<class\>	example_module/observer	By convention a model called Observer
\<method\>	customerLogin	PHP method name on Observer model

Table 4.8: Example event observer configuration nodes

We will see how exactly the values listed in the table are used in the following code segments.

```
if (false===$events[$eventName]) {
    continue;
} else {
    $event = new Varien_Event($args);
    $event->setName($eventName);
    $observer = new Varien_Event_Observer();
}
```

If no observer is configured for the event within the area of the current iteration, the loop continues with the next registered event area.

Otherwise, the code begins to prepare dispatching the event observer methods.

A Varien_Event object is instantiated as a container object.

The $args array which was passed into the dispatchEvent() method is passed on to the constructor.

Since `Varien_Event` extends from `Varien_Object` all arguments will be available via magic getters.

The `Varien_Event_Observer` object, which is instantiated next, is a second container instance.

Don't be confused by the class name - the **$observer** is not "our" observer object. It is simply another container object for the event arguments, just like the **$event** object.

Why a second container? I don't know, probably for historical reasons. Why the strange naming? Same reason. Look for the next Magento Trivia section for a possible explanation.

```
foreach ($events[$eventName]['observers'] as $obsName=>$obs) {
    $observer->setData(array('event'=>$event));
```

Now finally all configured observers are processed in another **foreach** loop.
The **$event** instance is passed to the **$observer** instance.

The container object **$observer** now contains the other container object **$event** which can be accessed using **$observer->getEvent()**.

Once again: that's history. :)

```
switch ($obs['type']) {
    case 'disabled':
        break;
    case 'object':
    case 'model':
        $method = $obs['method'];
        $observer->addData($args);
        $object = Mage::getModel($obs['model']);
        $this->_callObserverMethod($object, $method, $observer);
        break;
    default:
        $method = $obs['method'];
        $observer->addData($args);
        $object = Mage::getSingleton($obs['model']);
        $this->_callObserverMethod($object, $method, $observer);
        break;
    }
  }
}
```

```
    return $this;
}
```

Depending on the `<type>` node value, the real observer class - the one specified in the `<class>` node - is instantiated in a different fashion.

The following table shows the factory method that is used depending on the observer type.

Type Value	Factory Method	Comment
model	Mage::getModel()	-
object	Mage::getModel()	Generally not used, use model instead.
singleton	Mage::getSingleton()	The default if the `<type>` node is omitted
disabled	n.a.	The event observer is not instantiated

Table 4.9: Observer Instantiation Types

If the type is set to `disabled` the observer will be skipped.
This is useful to disable event observers declared by the core or other extensions.

The only reason to use a `singleton` type is if you want to maintain some kind of state information in the observer instance.

Note that the event arguments are also assigned to the `$observer` container, for both the `model` and `default` cases of the **switch** block: `$observer->addData($args)`.

This means that the event arguments can be accessed in many different ways from within the observer method.

For example, the argument to the event
`Mage::dispatchEvent('calculation_complete', array('the_answer' => 42))`
could be accessed in the following ways:

- `$observer->getData('the_answer'); // via Varien_Object::getData()`
- `$observer->getTheAnswer(); // via Varien_Object magic getter`
- `$observer->getEvent()->getData('the_answer');`
- `$observer->getEvent()->getTheAnswer();`

It doesn't make a difference which way you choose (except for the number of characters you type) - the result is always the same.

The one piece of information that is only available via the `Varien_Event` instance is the event name.

After the container objects have been prepared and the observer instance is created, finally the observer method is called:

```
protected function _callObserverMethod($object, $method, $observer)
{
    if (method_exists($object, $method)) {
        $object->$method($observer);
    } elseif (Mage::getIsDeveloperMode()) {
        Mage::throwException(
            'Method "'.$method.'" is not defined in "'.get_class($object).'"'
        );
    }
    return $this;
}
```

The `$observer` container object is passed as an argument to the configured observer method.

Within the Magento developer community it is common practice to choose event observer method names which match the event name, only in camel case so they match the coding standard.
For example, in the exercise solution, the observer for the event `controller_action_predispatch_cms_page_view` uses the method name `controllerActionPredispatchCmsPageView()`.

It is very convenient to immediately see what event triggers a given method while reading the observer class code.

The core team does not follow a clear convention though.
Some modules use method names that describe the method of the observer (for example `checkQuoteItemQty()`), while some use methods that match the event name (for example `sales_quote_address_discount_item()`).

This book recommends naming the observer methods like the event names they are triggered by (in camel case).

This completes the observer configuration discussion.

Please refer to the exercise solution file *app/code/local/Meeting02/RedirectToRoot/etc/config.xml* for the full exercise solution code of the observer configuration.

Exercise Solution Observer Method

The exercise solution observer method is quite small.

```
public function controllerActionPredispatchCmsPageView(
    Varien_Event_Observer $observer
)
{
    /* @var $action Mage_Cms_PageController */
    $action = $observer->getControllerAction();
    $pathInfo = $action->getRequest()->getPathInfo();
    list($homeCmsPage) = explode(
        '|', Mage::getStoreConfig('web/default/cms_home_page')
    );
    if (mb_strstr($pathInfo, "/$homeCmsPage") !== false) {
        $action->getResponse()->setRedirect(Mage::getBaseUrl());
        $action->setFlag(
            '', Mage_Core_Controller_Varien_Action::FLAG_NO_DISPATCH, true
        );
    }
}
```

Most of this code is rather self-explanatory after the extensive research chapter.

One thing which probably isn't clear on casual reading though is why the configuration setting is split using a | character.

The system configuration value that is read specifies the CMS page to display as the home page. It is compared against the current request path after the explode() function call. The question is, why is the value split at a pipe character?

The options of the system configuration select field are generated by the source model Mage_Adminhtml_Model_System_Config_Source_Cms_Page.

The cms/page title is used as the select label that is visible in the dropdown.
The cms/page identifier string is used for the option values.

However, cms/page identifiers are not globally unique.

It is possible to create two CMS pages with the same identifier, as long as they are assigned to different store views.

In that case, the CMS page selection source model values are qualified by appending the cms/page entity ID, separated by a |.

For example, if two CMS pages exist with the identifier no-route - one for the "All Stores" scope, and one for the "English" store view scope - the second one in the list will receive the cms page ID as the suffix.

Technically, the CMS page selection source model for the system configuration (adminhtml/system_config_source_cms_page) calls the method Mage_Cms_Model_Resource_Page_Collection::toOptionIdArray() method to generate the list of options, which is where the qualification with the page ID takes place.

```php
// Excerpt from Mage_Cms_Model_Resource_Page_Collection
public function toOptionIdArray()
{
    $res = array();
    $existingIdentifiers = array();
    foreach ($this as $item) {
        $identifier = $item->getData('identifier');

        $data['value'] = $identifier;
        $data['label'] = $item->getData('title');

        if (in_array($identifier, $existingIdentifiers)) {
            $data['value'] .= '|' . $item->getData('page_id');
        } else {
            $existingIdentifiers[] = $identifier;
        }

        $res[] = $data;
    }

    return $res;
}
```

That is the reason why the CMS home page identifier is split using a | character before it is compared against the current request path by the observer.

It might seem like a lot of effort to extract the name of the configured CMS home page. Lots of people simply hardcode "home" as the value to test against.

However, this course breaks if a different cms page were chosen, which is the case for default EE installation.

If the current request path starts with the configured CMS page identifier, a redirect to Magento base URL is set on the response object:

```
$action->getResponse()->setRedirect(Mage::getBaseUrl());
$action->setFlag(
    ", Mage_Core_Controller_Varien_Action::FLAG_NO_DISPATCH, true
);
```

Since the visitor will be redirected using a 302 HTTP response code and location header, the response body will not be displayed by the browser.
Because of that it would be a waste of server resources to generate some HTML content.

To tell the action controller to skip calling the actual action method, the `FLAG_NO_DISPATCH` flag is set on it.

Setting the flag to **true** will cause the response body to be empty, and no resources will be spent on loading and rendering the CMS page.

Magento Trivia

Besides the event observer system implemented in `Mage_Core_Model_App`, the `Mage` class also contains an alternative Event Observer implementation.

It is functional but is never used within the Magento framework.

Since it it part of the `Varien` library, it probably predates Magento.

In it observers are configured using the method
`Mage::addObserver($eventName, $callback, $args);`

To add all configured event observers for a specific area,
`Mage::getConfig()->loadEventObservers($areaCode)` can be used.

The configuration XML structure that is read is the same as for the `core/app` event observer implementation.

To fetch the `Varien_Event_Collection` with all observers, the method `Mage::getEvents()` is available.

In order to dispatch an event, `Mage::getEvents()->dispatch($eventCode, $args)` is called.

Since this never happens in the core code, it really is quite useless.

I'm only guessing here, but the convoluted `core/app` event observer argument container structure probably goes back to this implementation, where individual observers could be dispatched by calling `$observer->dispatch($event)`.

Chapter 5

Exercise: Custom frontend controller route; setting the response body

Original task description

The original task description from the study group kit for this exercise is as follows:

> Add a new frontend route and create an index controller and an index action that set the return value of `$this->getFullActionName()` to the response body.

Overview

This chapter discusses the following topics in the research section and the examination of the exercise solution:

- Action controller instantiation
- Route configuration

Scenario

Every time an extension adds a new page (aka "a route") to a Magento instance, a custom action controller is required.

Example scenarios which use a custom controller could be

- A Custom Frontend Search Form
- Custom Adminhtml Reports
- Custom REST API resources
- Payment Gateway Notification Target URLs
- And many many more. The list is endless...

Research

In the previous chapter the whole routing process was discussed in detail.

For every request the final situation of the routing process was that the `Standard` router dispatches an action controller method.

However, all that the chapter covered was that the standard router loads a list of configured routes. It did not discuss how the routes are configured.

Lets have a look at the method `Mage_Core_Controller_Varien_Router_Standard::collectRoutes()`, which is responsible for gathering all configured routes within the router area.

Just as a reminder: `collectRoutes()` is called from the Front Controller's `init()` method.

Since the `Admin` router inherits the `collectRoutes()` method from the `Standard` router through class inheritance, the `admin` and `frontend` routes share the configuration structure.

The only difference in the configuration XML structure between `Admin` and `Standard` routes is that the former go into the `<admin>` area, while the latter belong in the `<frontend>` config branch.[1]

This is the code that fetches the router configuration from the routers area:

---

[1] The area the routers are associated with are configured in the config XML branch `default/web/routers`. Please refer to the Front Controller Routing Process section of the previous chapter for details.

```
public function collectRoutes($configArea, $useRouterName)
{
    $routers = array();
    $routersConfigNode = Mage::getConfig()->getNode($configArea.'/routers');
    if($routersConfigNode) {
        $routers = $routersConfigNode->children();
    }
```

The variable **$routers** now contains an array with all the routes that are configured in the **<frontend>** or **<admin>** area respectively.

In the next step the router iterates over all those configured routes.

```
foreach ($routers as $routerName=>$routerConfig) {
    $use = (string)$routerConfig->use;
    if ($use == $useRouterName) {
```

Note that the value of the **<use>** node is compared with the value of **$useRouterName**, which was passed in as a method argument.

The value that was passed in as the **$useRouterName** is taken from the router configuration. Please refer to the Front Controller Routing Process section of the previous chapter for details.

The following (abbreviated) code is only executed if the value of the **<use>** node matches the router **$useRouterName** value.

```
    $modules = array((string)$routerConfig->args->module);
    if ($routerConfig->args->modules) {
        foreach ($routerConfig->args->modules->children() as $customModule) {
            if ($customModule) {
                $modules[] = (string)$customModule;
            }
        }
    }

    $frontName = (string)$routerConfig->args->frontName;
    $this->addModule($frontName, $modules, $routerName);
}
```

The **$modules** array is initialized with the value of the **<args><module>**... node.

Additional routes can be configured within the **<args><modules>**... branch. Each additional module is then also added to the **$modules** array.

This mostly happens for the `adminhtml` route. For example, if we try the following debug code at the end of the `collectRoutes()` method

```
if ('adminhtml' == $routerName) print_r($modules);
```

it displays a list of all modules which register themselves for the `adminhtml` route.

```
Array
(
    [0]  => Mage_Index_Adminhtml
    [1]  => Mage_Paygate_Adminhtml
    [2]  => Mage_Paypal_Adminhtml
    [3]  => Mage_Widget_Adminhtml
    [4]  => Mage_Oauth_Adminhtml
    [5]  => Mage_Authorizenet_Adminhtml
    [6]  => Mage_Bundle_Adminhtml
    [7]  => Mage_Centinel_Adminhtml
    [8]  => Mage_Compiler_Adminhtml
    [9]  => Mage_Connect_Adminhtml
    [10] => Mage_Downloadable_Adminhtml
    [11] => Mage_ImportExport_Adminhtml
    [12] => Mage_Api2_Adminhtml
    [13] => Mage_PageCache_Adminhtml
    [14] => Mage_XmlConnect_Adminhtml
    [15] => Mage_Adminhtml
    [16] => Phoenix_Moneybookers
)
```

However, in a non-customized Magento instance all the frontend routes only contain a single module.
Extensions however often add themselves to existing routes in this way.

Finally, almost at the end of the `collectRoutes()` method, this list of modules is added to the `Standard` router's internal map of `frontNames` to modules.

```
$this->addModule($frontName, $modules, $routerName);
```

Here is a frontend route configuration example from the `Mage_Catalog` module with some comments thrown in.

```
<!-- route area -->
<frontend>
    <routers>
        <!-- route name -->
        <catalog>
            <!-- the router name (standard or admin) -->
            <use>standard</use>
            <args>
                <!-- initial $modules entry -->
                <module>Mage_Catalog</module>
                <!-- first request path part -->
                <frontName>catalog</frontName>
            </args>
        </catalog>
    </routers>
</frontend>
```

Solution

The example solution code can be found in the extension `Meeting02_CustomController`.

The Route Configuration

The configuration for the custom route looks as follows:

```
<!-- route area -->
<frontend>
    <routers>
        <!-- route name -->
        <meeting02_customController>
            <!-- collected by the Standard router -->
            <use>standard</use>
            <args>
                <!-- map frontName to Meeting02_CustomController module -->
                <module>Meeting02_CustomController</module>
```

```
            <frontName>custom</frontName>
        </args>
    </meeting02_customController>
</routers>
</frontend>
```

The route is configured for the frontend area.

For the route name the module's namespace and name is used (as seen on line 3), which follows best practice, since it has to be a unique node.

The <use> value has to be standard so the Standard router will add this route to its list.

Then, the initial mapping from the frontName to a module is configured.

To be more precise, this code actually configures a mapping from a frontName *custom* to the Meeting02_CustomController's *controllers* directly.

Every time a browser sends a request with a matching first request path part, the Standard router will check in that directory for a matching controller.

The Action Controller Class

Examining the example solution's *controllers* directory, we can see there is an *IndexController.php* file.

As discussed in depth in the previous chapter, all files containing controller classes must end with the *Controller.php* suffix.

A request path for */custom/index* will cause the Standard router to check in this class for a matching action (the frontName *custom* and the controller name *index*).

Repeating another fact discussed in the last chapter, the class name of the controller almost follows the same conventions as modules and blocks, except that the *controllers* directory is omitted from the class name.

The full controller class from the sample exercise solution only has a couple of lines:

```
class Meeting02_CustomController_IndexController
    extends Mage_Core_Controller_Front_Action
{
    public function indexAction()
    {
```

```
        $this->getResponse()->setBody($this->getFullActionName());
    }
}
```

All frontend controllers have to extend from `Mage_Core_Controller_Front_Action`, so ours does too.

Since the controller is called `IndexController`, it will be used as the default if no controller name is specified in the request.

The only defined action method has the name `indexAction()`.

This means it will be called as the default action in case no action name was specified in the request path.

The sample solution action method can be called using any of the request paths from the following table:

Request Path	Comment
/custom/index/index	Full request path containing `frontName`, controller and action
/custom/index	Action name omitted
/custom	Controller and action name omitted

Table 5.1: Request paths dispatching the example solution controller

The full action name, which is set as the response object body within the `indexAction()` method, has also been discussed in the previous chapter in the context of the events dispatched in the action controller's `preDispatch()` method.

The return value consists of the current route name (`meeting02_customController`), the controller name (`index`) and the action name (also `index`).
For the sample exercise solution the output this gives us is
`meeting02_customController_index_index`.[2]

This completes the chapter.

---

[2]The full action name is also used as the layout action handle during the rendering of the view layer. However, for that use case it is converted to lower case.
This is discussed in detail in the next book of this series: Rendering and Widgets.

Chapter 6

Exercise: Action controller rewrite; customer/session before_auth_url property

Original task description

The original task description from the study group kit for this exercise is as follows:

> Rewrite the Mage_Customer_AccountController::loginAction() method to set a category view of your choice as the before_auth_url.

Overview

This chapter discusses the following topics in the research section and the examination of the exercise solution:

- The recommended way of doing controller rewrites
- The customer/session before_auth_url and after_auth_url properties

Scenario

There are several scenarios where redirecting the customer after login seems plausible:

- Alert the customer of a change in the terms-of-usage
- Notify the customer of a special promotion
- Ask the customer to complete the profile information

Admittedly, redirecting the customer to a category page doesn't really seem all that realistic, but it does serve as an educational example.
Maybe the category could have been prepared as a landing page for a special sale, right?

Research

So far several ways of rewriting requests where covered by this book.

- The DB based request rewrites applied by the Front Controller
- The config XML regular expression request rewrites, also applied by the Front Controller
- The config XML based rewrites applied by the action controller

Each of these could be used to route a request to a custom controller when the login page is requested, effectively implementing a controller rewrite.
But as you will recall, all methods but the DB based one are deprecated.

The database based URL rewrites are mainly used for mapping SEO URLs to internal routes.
Using the same functionality to implement a rewrite in a module would not be a clean solution.

Magento provides another mechanism that hasn't been covered yet for controller rewrites, and this method is the recommended way to implement them.

It utilizes the fact that a `frontName` can be mapped to more than module.
This feature was analyzed in depth in the exercise Custom frontend controller route; setting the response body.

To briefly reiterate: when the `Standard` (or `Admin`) router collects all configured routes, the mapping of the `frontName` to a module is initially done using the following configuration section.

```
<args>
    <!--
        map /example requests to controllers in Example/Module/controllers/
    -->
    <module>Example_Module</module>
    <frontName>example</frontName>
</args>
```

If additional modules are listed under the `args/modules` node - note the plural `<modules>` - then they are added to the list of possible matches, too.

The code sections which parse that configuration were discussed in the previous chapter. However, the code samples there were abbreviated.

To understand how this feature can be used to implement controller rewrites, having a look at the full code is necessary.
Here is the full route collection code from
`Mage_Core_Controller_Varien_Router_Standard::collectRoutes()`:

```
$modules = array((string)$routerConfig->args->module);
if ($routerConfig->args->modules) {
    foreach ($routerConfig->args->modules->children() as $customModule) {
        if ($customModule) {
            if ($before = $customModule->getAttribute('before')) {
                $position = array_search($before, $modules);
                if ($position === false) {
                    $position = 0;
                }
                array_splice($modules, $position, 0, (string)$customModule);
            } elseif ($after = $customModule->getAttribute('after')) {
                $position = array_search($after, $modules);
                if ($position === false) {
                    $position = count($modules);
                }
                array_splice($modules, $position+1, 0, (string)$customModule);
            } else {
                $modules[] = (string)$customModule;
```

```
            }
        }
    }
}
```

The initial `frontName`-to-module mapping is created right in the first line of the code block above.
The rest of the code iterates over all additional modules for the route currently being processed.

The difference from the previously discussed - abbreviated - version of the method is that the additional modules are not simply appended to `$modules`.

Instead, what happens depends on the presence or absence of a `before` or `after` attribute on the XML node.

In case a `before` node is present, the new module will be added to the list of modules before a record with the attributes value (see the first `if` branch).

In case an `after` node is present, the new module will be added after a record with the attribute value (see the `elseif` branch).

In case there is neither a `before` or an `after` node, the new module will simply be appended to the list (see the `else` branch above).

Let's go over a few examples to make things clearer.

Let's assume the following route configuration is present in the merged configuration XML:

```
<admin>
  <routers>
    <adminhtml>
      <use>admin</use>
      <args>
        <module>Mage_Adminhtml</module>
        <frontName>admin</frontName>
        <modules>
          <Mage_Paypal
              before="Mage_Adminhtml">Mage_Paypal_Adminhtml</Mage_Paypal>
          <widget
              before="Mage_Adminhtml">Mage_Widget_Adminhtml</widget>
          <moneybookers
              after="Mage_Adminhtml">Phoenix_Moneybookers</moneybookers>
```

```
        <example_mod
            before="Mage_Widget_Adminhtml">Example_Module_Adminhtml</example_mod>
        </modules>
        </args>
      </adminhtml>
  </routers>
</admin>
```

What will the final **$modules** array look like?

Let's go through step by step. Please make sure you follow why the array is build the way it is, referring to the code from the collectRoutes() method above.

1. The list is initialized with the original module as

   ```
   array('Mage_Adminhtml')
   ```

2. The Mage_Paypal module is added next, **before** the original record. Now the array contains two modules:

   ```
   array(
       'Mage_Paypal_Adminhtml',
       'Mage_Adminhtml'
   )
   ```

   Note that the value added to the array is the **node value**, not the node name.

3. The widget module is added before Mage_Adminhtml, in effect putting it between the first two records.

   ```
   array(
       'Mage_Paypal_Adminhtml',
       'Mage_Widget_Adminhtml',
       'Mage_Adminhtml'
   )
   ```

4. Then the moneybookers module is added **after** Mage_Adminhtml.
   The list of modules is getting longer:

   ```
   array(
       'Mage_Paypal_Adminhtml',
       'Mage_Widget_Adminhtml',
       'Mage_Adminhtml',
       'Phoenix_Moneybookers'
   )
   ```

5. The final node `example_mod` is unusual. It doesn't refer to the `Mage_Adminhtml` module, instead it refers to the `Mage_Widget_Adminhtml` module already in the array.

   It will be added before the other module accordingly:

```
array(
    'Mage_Paypal_Adminhtml',
    'Example_Module_Adminhtml',
    'Mage_Widget_Adminhtml',
    'Mage_Adminhtml',
    'Phoenix_Moneybookers'
)
```

For this example, this would be the full list of modules that the router would look inside for a matching controller.

Remember, each of those records is mapped to a directory in the module.
In this example, the router would look in the following directories until it finds a matching controller class:[1]

1. *Mage/Paypal/controllers/Adminhtml/*
2. *Example/Module/controllers/Adminhtml/*
3. *Mage/Widget/controllers/Adminhtml/*
4. *Mage/Adminhtml/controllers/*
5. *Phoenix/Moneybookers/controllers/*

This works just like the PHP include path.
The router looks into each of these directories in turn for the controller file and includes the first match it finds.

The controller file name the router looks for is built from the second part of the request path (the controller name) by appending *Controller.php* to it.

For sake of this example, let's assume the current request is for */admin/ajax*. In this case the controller name would be *ajax*.
The resulting controller file name would be *AjaxController.php*.

The router will look in each of the listed directories and use the first occurrence of *AjaxController.php* it finds.

---

[1]Just to reiterate: the *controllers* directory is inserted after the second part, so for example `Mage_Widget_Adminhtml` maps to the directory *Mage/Widget/controllers/Adminhtml*.

The router will only dispatch the controller if it has a matching action method, otherwise it will continue looking for another match.

In fact, the Magento core code contains a *Mage/Adminhtml/controllers/AjaxController.php* file.
Will this be the class file loaded?

Usually yes. But what if a controller file with the same name would have been added to a module earlier in the list?

In that case the controller from the module further up in the array would be used (if that controller contains a matching action).

This is the recommended way to implement controller rewrites.

To surmise, this feature can be used in two ways:

1. Add new controllers to an existing route (aka `frontName`)
2. Rewrite existing controllers

Adding new controllers is used mostly in the context of the `admin` area.

Controller rewrites are used for both the `frontend` and the `admin` area.

This type of controller rewrite can be very useful, but suffers the same downside as module, block, or helper class rewrites: each class can only be rewritten once.
If two modules try to rewrite the same controller, only one of them will be used.
The other one will be silently ignored, which can lead to confusing and maybe hard to debug behavior (*"Why is my controller rewrite not working?!?!"*).

When adding a new controller to an existing route, usually it is a good idea to use the `after` argument with the original module name, so if a module with the same name is added to the core in future, your module won't accidentally be masking it.

However, when rewriting a controller class, `before` has to be used in the configuration, otherwise the rewrite won't work if your route is added to the list after the rewrite target.

When implementing a controller rewrite, the new controller usually extends the original controller class.

Because controller classes are included by the router and not by the autoloader, simply defining the inheritance in PHP is not enough.

For action controllers we have to revert to manually specifying the class file to include, before it can be used as the parent in the class definition.[2]

The best way to build the path to the original controller class is using the `Mage::getModuleDir()` method.[3]

```php
<?php

$controllerDir = Mage::getModuleDir('controllers', 'Mage_Customer');
require_once $controllerDir . '/AccountController.php';

class Example_Module_Customer_AccountController
    extends Mage_Customer_AccountController {
```

Controller class files are the only classes of the Magento framework that are not included by the autoloader (besides `Mage`).

This section of the book now completes the whole routing process, starting with the Front Controller instantiating all routers, router matching and router delegation, the `Standard` router mapping the request to a route, instantiation of an action controller and finally the action controller being dispatched.

Magento Trivia: the Adminhtml 404 page

This chapter stated that when adding new *controllers* directories to a route, the configuration should use the `after` argument for new controllers, and `before` when rewriting a controller.

However, when adding new controllers to the `adminhtml` route, `before="Mage_Adminhtml"` should always be used instead of `after="Mage_Adminhtml"`.

This should be done for new controllers as well as rewrites.

Some might consider the reason for this to be a bug in Magento. Let's start with a little background information.

---

[2]To reiterate: the reason controller classes are not loaded by the autoloader is that the *controllers* directory isn't part of the class name and - even if it would be - the first character of *controllers* is lowercase.

[3]Some developers still prefer to use the `DIRECTORY_SEPARATOR` or `DS` constants as path separators instead of simply writing / before the file name, but since PHP will take care of automatically using the correct separator independently of what we specify, it doesn't have any benefit (except making the code harder to read).

The `Mage_Adminhtml` module implements its own 404 page.

It is used if the requested `frontName` matches a route that is registered with the `Admin` router, but no matching controller or action is found.

In that case, the router will not pass the request on to the `Standard` router to look for a match.

Instead, if no matching controller is found, the `Admin` router simply sets `$controller = 'index'` and `$action = 'noroute'`, and used that route to display the 404 page.

This case only happens if all modules in the array for the current route were already checked for a match. Because of that the variable `$realModule` contains the last value from that list.

That means the `Admin` router expects the last module in the list to contain an *IndexController.php* with a `norouteAction()` method.

The `Mage_Adminhtml` module contains a *IndexController.php* file with a `norouteAction()` method.

However, if there is a custom module in the list **after `Mage_Adminhtml`**, chances are it does not contain such a class.

In that case Magento simply falls back to checking the next router for a match after all.

The Magento Adminhtml 404 page has been broken for a long time.

The reason is that the `Phoenix_Moneybookers` module adds itself to the `adminhtml` route, **after `Mage_Adminhtml`**.

If you want to see the original admin 404 page, all you have to do is open the file *app/code/community/Phoenix/Moneybookers/etc/config.xml*, find the `admin` router section, and change `after="Mage_Adminhtml"` to `before="Mage_Adminhtml"`.

Then access a non-existant admin route, for example */admin/show-me-the-404-page*.

However - before you go ahead an try it out - it might not even be worth it. The `Mage_Adminhtml` 404 page does not look very special at all.

In case you want to look it up, the code in question can be found in `Mage_Core_Controller_Varien_Router_Admin::_noRouteShouldBeApplied()` and `Mage_Core_Controller_Varien_Router_Standard::match()`.

Remember that the `Admin` router extends the `Standard` router. Searching for the string `_noRouteShouldBeApplied` quickly lets you find the right code section.

Request Rewrite Summary

Before we wrap up this section, let's summarize all options Magento provides to apply controller rewrites:

#	Method	Applied in	Method	Use for
1	DB based (table `core_url_rewrite`)	Front Controller	`dispatch()`	SEO URLs
2	Config XML based (regular expression)	Front Controller	`dispatch()`	Deprecated
3	Config XML based	Action Controller	`preDispatch()`	Deprecated
4	Route to modules map	`Standard` Router	`match()`	Controller Rewrites

Table 6.1: Possibilities to rewrite requests in Magento

For the current exercise option number 4 will be the right choice to rewrite the `Mage_Customer_AccountController` controller.

But before we move on to the solution, there is one more little bit of useless Magento trivia for you if you enjoy that kind of thing.

Magento Trivia

The `Standard` router contains yet another rewrite implementation, but fortunately that `Mage_Core_Controller_Varien_Router_Standard::rewrite()` method is never called. It has been around since the first release of Magento, but it looks like it has long since been forgotten.

Solution

The example solution code can be found in the extension Meeting02_ControllerRewrite.

The *config.xml* code consists of two parts.

```
<?xml version="1.0"?>
<config>
  <frontend>
    <routers>
      <customer>
        <args>
          <modules>
            <meeting02_controllerRewrite
before="Mage_Customer">Meeting02_ControllerRewrite_Customer</meeting02_controllerRewrite>
          </modules>
        </args>
      </customer>
    </routers>
  </frontend>
  <default>
    <meeting02>
      <controller_rewrite>
        <target_category_id>22</target_category_id>
      </controller_rewrite>
    </meeting02>
  </default>
</config>
```

The first part between the **<routers>** node adds `Meeting02_ControllerRewrite_Customer` to the list of modules for the `customer` route.

Since we want to implement a rewrite, the attribute `before="Mage_Customer"` has to be specified.

When a request matching the `customer` route's `frontName` is received, this will cause the `Standard` router to look for a matching controller in the directory *Meeting02/ControllerRewrite/controllers/Customer/*, **before** it looks in the `Mage_Customer` module.

Please note that the indentation for the node **<meeting02_controllerRewrite>** is strange because no whitespace is allowed around the value.
If you (or your IDE) adds newlines or spaces, the rewrite will simply not work.
Who knows, maybe a `trim()` will be added in the future - it's never too late to dream (or submit a patch).

The second part of the configuration within the **<default>** branch specifies the category ID to which a customer should be redirected after a successful login.

Since the configuration already has been discussed in detail in the research section of this chapter, let's move on to the controller code of the example exercise solution.

```
require_once Mage::getModuleDir('controllers', 'Mage_Customer') .
    '/AccountController.php';

class Meeting02_ControllerRewrite_Customer_AccountController
    extends Mage_Customer_AccountController
{
```

The parent class is manually included before the class declaration, since the Magento autoloader will not include it (as already discussed earlier in this chapter).

The new class then can extend from the original rewritten class without PHP complaining about the unknown class.

The new class overwrites the parent's **loginAction()** method and adds one new method of its own.

```
    public function loginAction()
    {
        parent::loginAction();

        $categoryId = Mage::getStoreConfig(
            'meeting02/controller_rewrite/target_category_id'
        );
        $storeId = Mage::app()->getStore()->getId();
        $url = $this->_getSeoCategoryUrl($categoryId, $storeId);
        $this->_getSession()->setBeforeAuthUrl($url);
    }
```

Before anything else is done, the **parent::loginAction()** method is called. This keeps the code as upgrade-safe as possible, since any future changes will probably be picked up automatically - no code was copied and pasted from the parent method.

To generate the target URL a custom method **_getSeoCategoryUrl()** is used - we will look at that next. The returned URL is then set on the **customer/session** model using the magic setter **setBeforeAuthUrl()**.

```
    protected function _getSeoCategoryUrl($categoryId, $storeId)
    {
        $requestPath = Mage::getResourceSingleton('core/url_rewrite')
            ->getRequestPathByIdPath('category/' . $categoryId, $storeId);

        if ($requestPath) {
            $url = Mage::getModel('core/url')->getDirectUrl($requestPath);
        } else {
            $url = Mage::getModel('core/url')->getUrl(
                'catalog/category/view', array('id' => $categoryId)
            );
        }
        return $url;
    }
}
```

In the method _getSeoCategoryUrl() it is first attempted to load the search engine friendly URL for the given category ID.
If that fails it falls back to the internal URL path */catalog/category/view/id/22*.

The method calls to `Mage_Core_Model_Url` serve to add the configured base URL to the request path.

In the **if** branch of the code block above, the method `getDirectUrl()` leaves the request path as it is. Additional parameters passed as a second argument will be ignored, the only thing it does is it prefixes the path with the store's base URL.

On the other hand, if the request path consists of the route name, controller, and action, it has to be passed through `getUrl()` (refer to the **else** branch).

It will replace the first part - the route name - with the matching `frontName` and then prefix the result with the store's base URL.

Any parameters passed as the second argument to the method will be added to the request path.

The customer session before_ and after_auth_url

If the `customer/session` model `before_auth_url` and `after_auth_url` properties are set, they are used to determine the page a customer is redirected to after login.

This happens in the method
`Mage_Customer_AccountController::_loginPostRedirect()`.

The method is surprisingly complex.[4]

The details aren't relevant for the certification.
I'll only go into the specifics below so it may be used as a reference for work if needed.

The gist of it is that `after_auth_url` is only evaluated if the authentication was successful, that is, when the customer logged in successfully.
If it isn't set or the login wasn't successful, the `before_auth_url` is used.

There also is a configuration option that influences the redirect target if the login was successful under some conditions.
The setting can be found at *Customer Configuration > Login Options > Redirect Customer to Account Dashboard after Logging in.*

The following table describes most cases that can occur.

before set	after set	Login okay	Config option set	Redirect target
yes	yes	yes	-	`after_auth_url`
yes	no	yes	-	`before_auth_url`
no	yes	yes	no	`after_auth_url`
no	no	yes	no	Account Page
no	yes	yes	yes	`referer` or Account Page
no	no	yes	yes	`referer` or Account Page
yes	yes	no	-	`before_auth_url`
yes	no	no	-	`before_auth_url`
no	yes	no	-	Login Page
no	no	no	-	Login Page

Table 6.2: Possible post login URL redirect targets

There still are two special cases that aren't included in the table that I'll just mention for sake of completeness.

---

[4]The cyclomatic complexity number of the `Mage_Customer_AccountController::_loginPostRedirect()` method is 11, even though it only consists of 39 lines of code!

1. When the `before_auth_url` equals the base URL it is not used. The behavior is just as if `before_auth_url` isn't set at all.

2. If the `before_auth_url` equals the logout page URL it is changed to the customer account page.

The `before_auth_url` property is set in many places within the Magento core. The `after_auth_url` property usually isn't set.

The usual flow is the following:

- A page requires the customer to be logged in, so it calls `Mage::getModel('customer/session')->setBeforeAuthUrl($url)` before it redirects the customer to the login page (`$url` is the URL of the protected page).

- After the customer then attempts to log in, he is redirected back to the `before_auth_url`, regardless of whether the login attempt succeeded or not.

- In case the customer did not log in, he will be redirected to the login form again.

- If the login was successful, the customer now is able to view the protected page.

Use `$session->setAfterAuthUrl($url)` to force the customer to be redirected to a specific URL after a successful login.

In the Magento core the `after_auth_url` property is rarely set, so it is an ideal candidate for customizations.[5]

When setting the `after_auth_url` session property be aware that it also affects customer logins during the checkout (which uses the `before_auth_url` property to redirect the customers back to the checkout after authorization).

---

[5]Only the `Mage_Oauth_AuthorizeController` class sets the `after_auth_url` property. However, it is set to the customer login URL.
I leave it to the reader to decide if it makes sense to redirect the customer to the login page after a successful authorization.

Chapter 7

Exercise: Dynamic class rewrites

Original task description

The original task description from the study group kit for this exercise is as follows:

> Create a dynamic rewrite of the `payment/data` helper only if the version of Magento is older than version 1.4, and if the ccsave payment option is enabled for the current store.

Overview

This chapter discusses the following topics in the research section and the examination of the exercise solution:

- Reading and setting configuration settings (both scoped and unscoped)
- Saving configuration settings

Scenario

The idea behind this exercise is very useful. Being able to dynamically set configuration
values enables many customizations, mostly using observers, that otherwise would require
a class rewrite or other much more invasive code.

For example, it can be used for:

- Providing backward compatibility for modules by rewriting a class only under specific
  circumstances
- Enabling and disabling payment methods and shipping carriers on the fly
- Working around method signature changes between Magento versions (for example,
  if a method used to be `private` and now is `protected`)[1]
- Creating config fixtures for unit tests

Any configurable value can be set this way, making it an extremely powerful technique.

Research

Let's start by having a look at how configuration values are read, because then it will
become obvious how they are set.

Reading Configuration Values

In Magento there basically are two ways configuration values are accessed.

- Scoped values (mainly used for system configuration settings) accessed via
  `Mage_Core_Model_Store::getConfig()`
- General configuration values accessed via
  `Mage_Core_Model_Config::getNode()`

---

[1]**Magento Trivia**:   an   example   for   a   change   in   method   visibility   is
`Mage_Catalog_Model_Product_Image::_rgbToString()` which used to be `private` up until Magento 1.4.1,
when it was changed to `protected`.

Scoped Configuration Values

A scoped configuration value is a setting that can be defined in one or more scopes.
There are three scopes:

Scope	Priority
default	Lowest priority
website	Overrides default scope values
store	Overrides default and website scope values

Table 7.1: Configuration scopes

If a value is set in more than one scope, the more specific scope value will override the less specific one.

Please refer to the next chapter on the dispatch process for details on how the configuration is loaded.

To access scoped values usually the static `Mage::getStoreConfig()` or `Mage::getStoreConfigFlag()` methods are used.

They automatically return the value from the most specific scope for the specified path.

The two methods of the `Mage` class fetch the current (or the specified) store model and then use `$store->getConfig()` to access the scoped value.

The `Mage_Core_Model_Store` class `getConfig()` method looks like this:

```
public function getConfig($path)
{
    if (isset($this->_configCache[$path])) {
        return $this->_configCache[$path];
    }

    $config = Mage::getConfig();

    $fullPath = 'stores/' . $this->getCode() . '/' . $path;
    $data = $config->getNode($fullPath);
```

```
    if (!$data) {
        return null;
    }
    return $this->_processConfigValue($fullPath, $path, $data);
}
```

We can see that the value is cached on the store model once it is accessed, so subsequent calls with the same path will return the cached value.

When trying to change values on the fly it is important to considering caching, so let's keep that in mind while we explore further.

In case a non-true value was returned by **$config->getNode()**, the method returns **null**.

However, if a value evaluating to true was returned, it is passed through _processConfigValue() before the value is returned (at the end of the code block above). The method _processConfigValue() contains two little-known features.

Lets have a closer look at it.

```
protected function _processConfigValue($fullPath, $path, $node)
{
```

Just for reference: the variable **$fullPath** contains the full XPath to the configuration setting including the store scope prefix.

The variable **$path** contains the config path without any scope applied.

The **$node** variable contains the Mage_Core_Model_Config_Element node returned by **$config->getNode()**

Let's inspect the next part of the _processConfigValue() method.

```
    if ($node->hasChildren()) {
        $aValue = array();
        foreach ($node->children() as $k => $v) {
            $aValue[$k] = $this->_processConfigValue(
                $fullPath . '/' . $k, $path . '/' . $k, $v
            );
        }
        $this->_configCache[$path] = $aValue;
        return $aValue;
    }
```

The above section of code builds the content for the already mentioned configuration cache property.

If the requested node has children, the values of all branches below the requested node are cached as an array.

Not a lot we can do with that.

The next section of the method is more useful:

```
$sValue = (string) $node;
if (!empty($node['backend_model']) && !empty($sValue)) {
    $backend = Mage::getModel((string) $node['backend_model']);
    $backend->setPath($path)->setValue($sValue)->afterLoad();
    $sValue = $backend->getValue();
}
```

First the node value is cast to a string. Up until now it still was a `Mage_Core_Model_Config_Element` instance.[2]

And here we discover a little-known feature: any scoped configuration value may have a backend model.

If a `backend_model="..."` argument is present, the model is instantiated, the config value is set on it, then `afterLoad()` is called, and the returned value is used after that.

This functionality might be used for many things:

- mapping ID values to labels
- translation
- processing placeholders
- loading the contents of files specified in the configuration value

That list surely is very incomplete but hopefully is enough to trigger your own ideas on how to use it.

Getting back to the `_processConfigValue()` method, some further processing of the string value happens next:

---

[2]The `Mage_Core_Model_Config_Element` is just a relatively small wrapper around `Varien_Simplexml_Element`, which in turn extends the standard PHP `SimpleXmlElement` class.

```
if (is_string($sValue) && strpos($sValue, '{{') !== false) {
    if (strpos($sValue, '{{unsecure_base_url}}') !== false) {
        $unsecureBaseUrl = $this->getConfig(self::XML_PATH_UNSECURE_BASE_URL);
        $sValue = str_replace(
            '{{unsecure_base_url}}', $unsecureBaseUrl, $sValue
        );
    } elseif (strpos($sValue, '{{secure_base_url}}') !== false) {
        $secureBaseUrl = $this->getConfig(self::XML_PATH_SECURE_BASE_URL);
        $sValue = str_replace('{{secure_base_url}}', $secureBaseUrl, $sValue);
    } elseif (strpos($sValue, '{{base_url}}') !== false) {
        $sValue = Mage::getConfig()->substDistroServerVars($sValue);
    }
}
```

Configuration values can contain references to the configured secure or unsecure base URL (see the if or the first elseif branches.).

However, the most interesting one is the last placeholder option: {{base_url}} (in the second elseif condition branch).

If the string {{base_url}} is present in the config value, the config model's method substDistroServerVars() replaces it with the currently requested host name (including the *http* or *https* schema).

If the store code is configured to be part of the request path, it will **not** be included in the {{base_url}} replacement value.

The remainder of the _processConfigValue() method simply sets the store's config cache property for the current path and returns the final value:

```
    $this->_configCache[$path] = $sValue;

    return $sValue;
}
```

Magento Trivia

The method Mage_Core_Model_Config::substDistroServerVars() actually does a str_replace() on more than just the {{base_url}}, even though that string has to be present in the config value to trigger the replacement method call.

The method will also process the following placeholders if present in the config value:

Placeholder	Replacement
{{root_dir}}	Magento base directory
{{app_dir}}	Magento base directory + /app
{{var_dir}}	Magento base directory + /var
{{base_url}}	Currently requested base URL

Table 7.2: `substDistroServerVars()` placeholders

Since the {{base_url}} placeholder has to be present in the config value to trigger the automatic replacement, the other values will probably never be useful.

Unless, of course, you call `Mage::getConfig()->substDistroServerVars($string)` yourself, passing in a string containing any of the four placeholders.

However, when referring to the other directories in custom code, it is much more common to call `Mage::getBaseDir()`, with the appropriate type as an argument.

Back from the Magento Trivia section.

As mentioned earlier, instead of calling `getConfig()` directly on the store model, most developers use `Mage::getStoreConfig()`.

Mage::getStoreConfig($path, $store = null)

This method directly returns the value from `$store->getConfig()`. Unless a specific store code, ID, or model is passed as an argument, the current store view is used.

Mage::getStoreConfigFlag($path, $store = null)

This method takes the return value of `Mage::getStoreConfig()` and returns it as a boolean.
But instead of using PHP to simply typecast the value, `getStoreConfigFlag()` does the conversion itself.

The result is the same as if

```
return (bool) Mage::getStoreConfig($path, $store);
```

would have been used.

However, there is one *magentoism* to watch out for when using `Mage::getStoreConfigFlag()`:

If the config node value were the string `false` - which would be cast to **true** by PHP - it returns the boolean **false** instead.

Unscoped Configuration Values

The scoped configuration is only a small subsection of the overall Magento configuration. To access an arbitrary node within the config DOM structure, the method `Mage_Core_Model_Config::getNode()` is used.

Since the XML processing in Magento is based on PHP's SimpleXml[3], the request paths always are in the context of a node.

Usually this is the root node, `<config>`, which means this node is omitted when specifying a config path.

For example, given the following XML tree:

```
<config>
    <modules>
        <Mage_Log>
            <active>true</active>
            <codePool>local</codePool>
        </Mage_Log>
    </modules>
</config>
```

to read the value of the `<codePool>` node, the method call would need to be :

```
$codePool = (string) Mage::getConfig()->getNode('modules/Mage_Log/codePool');
```

The path is `modules/Mage_Log/codePool` without the `<config>` node at the beginning.

Note that the returned value of `getNode()` is a `Mage_Core_Model_Config_Element` instance, so it might need to be cast to a string.

---

[3]http://php.net/manual/en/book.simplexml.php

If the requested path doesn't exist, the return value of `getNode()` is **false**.

It is very important to be attentive to the casing of the XML path expression.

The nodes `codepool` and `codePool` would be completely different, even if they share the same parent node.

Setting Configuration Values

Coming back to the exercise at hand, we still have to see how configuration values can be specified dynamically on the fly.

Setting Scoped Configuration Values

Since scoped values are accessed via the store model, they should also be set that way. The `Mage_Core_Model_Store` class offers the method `setConfig()` for this purpose.

```
public function setConfig($path, $value)
{
    if (isset($this->_configCache[$path])) {
        $this->_configCache[$path] = $value;
    }
    $fullPath = 'stores/' . $this->getCode() . '/' . $path;
    Mage::getConfig()->setNode($fullPath, $value);

    return $this;
}
```

The reason it is important to use this method instead of simply setting the value on the `core/config` singleton is that it takes care of updating the configuration cache property in the store model.

In case the config value was previously accessed through the `core/store` model, simply changing the node value in the `core/config` singleton would not be enough, since the `$_configCache` store property would mask the changes.

Setting Unscoped Configuration Values

The store model's `setConfig()` method already shows us how generic configuration values are set.

```
Mage::getConfig()->setNode($path, $value);
```

Note the value will not be saved to the database or even the Magento cache backend. It is only valid for the duration of the current request.

This is exactly what we need for the this chapter's exercise, which is to dynamically implement a class rewrite.

Before we move on to the solution, let's have a look at saving configuration values.

Persisting Configuration Values

Even though it is not required for the current exercise, it is useful to know how to persist configuration values.

Saving Scoped Configuration Values

Any scoped value can be persisted in the `core_config_data` table. There are several ways to accomplish that (besides resorting to plain SQL).

For example, let's assume we want to set the value for `general/locale/code` to `uk_UA` (Ukrainian) on a store view scope for the store with the ID 3.

Let's examine three ways this can be done.

The first one is to use the `core/config` singleton:

```
// In any context
Mage::getConfig()->saveConfig('general/locale/code', 'uk_UA', 'stores', 3);
```

The method signature looks like this:

```
public function saveConfig($path, $value, $scope = 'default', $scopeId = 0)
```

The second way to store scoped configuration values is to use the `core/config_data` model:

```
// In any context
Mage::getModel('core/config_data')
    ->setScope('stores')
    ->setScopeId(3)
    ->setPath('general/locale/code')
    ->setValue('uk_UA')
    ->save();
```

Any existing value for the specified path and scope would automatically be replaced, even if the model wasn't previously loaded.

The third and final way to save scoped config values is mostly used within setup scripts:

```
// In setup scripts
$installer->setConfigData('general/locale/code', 'uk_UA', 'stores', 3);
```

All setup classes inherit this method from `Mage_Core_Model_Resource_Setup`.

The method signature is identical to the one of the `core/config` class (except for the method name).

In the end it doesn't matter which of these methods you choose - the end result is the same.

Saving Unscoped Configuration Values

The Magento core doesn't provide a mechanism to save unscoped configuration values.

The only way to accomplish that would be to write them to an XML file, which is then merged into the config DOM on subsequent requests.

If you ever find yourself in the need for doing that, chances are there is a better approach then saving arbitrary config XML.
However, let's explore how it might be accomplished nevertheless.

Since the installation requires the *app/etc/* directory to be writable for creating the *app/etc/local.xml* file, writing a file there would probably work on many installations.

The file would also automatically be parsed and included in the configuration DOM during the loading of the base configuration.

However, it probably isn't a good idea, since any security-aware webmaster should restrict write access to that directory again after the Magento installation is complete.

So how about writing the XML to a file in a subdirectory of *media/* or *var/*, and manually merge it into the loaded configuration?

That would certainly be possible. Making it work with more then a single webserver would be more challenging though.

Probably it would be better to revise your module's architecture to use regular entity storage tables instead.

Solution

The example solution code can be found in the extension `Meeting02_DynamicRewrite`.

The entry point for the module logic is an event observer for the `controller_front_init_before` event.

As discussed in the observer section of the "redirect to base URL chapter", that event is triggered very early during every dispatch.

It is a good point to do dynamic config changes, since chances are that the evaluation of the configuration values in question hasn't taken place yet.

When choosing this event to do dynamic class rewrites, one thing to watch out for is that the rewrite will only be applied if Magento is processing a request.

If the Magento runtime environment is initialized from a cron script or a custom command line script, the Front Controller will not be dispatched, and thus the event will not be fired.

The observer method in exercise solution's class `Meeting02_DynamicRewrite_Model_Observer` looks as follows:

```
public function controllerFrontInitBefore(Varien_Event_Observer $observer)
{
    $store = $this->_getStore();
    if ($store->getConfig('payment/ccsave/active')) {
        $helper = $this->_getHelper();
        $helper->rewritePaymentHelperIfAncient();
    }
}
```

Adhering to best practices, the observer delegates the main work to a model, or in this case, a helper. The method is `Meeting02_DynamicRewrite_Helper_Data::rewritePaymentHelperIfAncient()`:

```
public function rewritePaymentHelperIfAncient()
{
    $this->setConfigIfVersion(
        '1.4', // compare Magento against
        '<',        // comparison operator
        'global/helpers/payment/rewrite/data', // rewrite config path
        'Meeting02_DynamicRewrite_Helper_Payment_Data' // rewrite value
    );
}

public function setConfigIfVersion($version, $comp, $path, $value)
{
    if (version_compare($this->_getMageVersion(), $version, $comp)) {
        $config = $this->_getConfig();
        $config->setNode($path, $value);
    }
}
```

According to the method, an ancient version is anything older than Magento version 1.4.

In that case, the config value `Meeting02_DynamicRewrite_Helper_Payment_Data` is set for the config path `global/helpers/payment/rewrite/data` using `setNode()` on the `core/config` model.[4]

In the replacement class for the payment helper, the filtering of available payment providers can take place for Magento versions older than 1.4.

The reason the rewrite only needs to be done in Magento versions older then 1.4 is because since then payment provider filtering can be done using an observer for the event `payment_method_is_active`, which is dispatched in `Mage_Payment_Model_Method_Abstract::isAvailable()`.

This completes the exercise solution code discussion.

Before finishing this chapter, please note that payment method availability could also be altered by setting the configuration node values of the payment method's `<active>` setting to `false`.

This is an alternative way to achieve the same result - filtering available payment methods - which would not require a class rewrite in any Magento version.

---

[4]The helper class `Meeting02_DynamicRewrite_Helper_Data` uses a getter method instead of calling `Mage::getConfig()` directly because it implements optional constructor injection in order to increase the testability.

On the other hand, it might be more difficult to find a good event candidate where all required information is available that is needed decide if a payment method should be active or not.

Here is an example of how a payment method could be deactivated using this approach:

```
$store = Mage::app()->getStore();
if (version_compare(Mage::getVersion(), '1.4', '<')) {
    $store->setConfig('payment/ccsave/active', false);
}
```

Chapter 8

Exercise: Diagram of the dispatch process

The original task description from the study group kit for this exercise is as follows:

> Create a diagram of the important classes involved in a request dispatch.

Overview

This chapter discusses the following topics in the research section and the examination of the exercise solution:

- A brief comparison of `Mage` vs. `Mage_Core_Model_App`
- Configuration XML merging
- Configuration XML load order
- The Application Dispatch Process

Scenario

Since this chapters exercise doesn't require writing any code, there really is no scenario for it.

Having a solid understanding of the Magento dispatch process of course is very valuable while debugging and when customizing Magento.

Research

This exercise gives us the opportunity to have a look at one very important aspect of Magento which we haven't covered so far: the configuration load process.

But before the configuration is loaded, a few even more basic elements of the Magento framework have to be initialized.

The very first step is including the file *app/Mage.php*, which sets up the autoloader and the include path.

But that alone isn't enough to initialize Magento. The next step is to prepare the Magento runtime environment.

Mage vs. Mage::app()

There are two ways the Magento runtime environment is initialized after the file *app/Mage.php* is included:

Initilazation Method	Purpose
`Mage::run()`	Sets up the Magento runtime environment and processes the current browser request.
`Mage::app()`	Just sets up the Magento runtime environment. No request processing is done. This is mostly used within custom command line scripts.

Table 8.1: Magento initialization

Either way, inside the `Mage` class the static property
`self::$_app = new Mage_Core_Model_App();` is set first.

The difference between the static `Mage` class and the instance returned by `Mage::app()` is a little confusing to some people.

The `Mage` class could be called a *god* class.
It is used all over the Magento codebase mainly for accessing the two most important objects of the framework: `Mage::getConfig()` and `Mage::app()`.

It also provides most of the factory methods, for example `Mage::getModel()` and `Mage::helper()`.

The special method `Mage::run()` starts the Magento dispatch process after initializing the runtime environment.

Also the `Mage` class is the home of the Magento registry.[1]

On the other hand, the `Mage_Core_Model_App` instance generally is used to access most of the request specific object instances within the Magento framework.

These include but are not limited to:

- The request and response objects
  (`Mage::app()->getRequest()` and `Mage::app()->getResponse()`)
- All store models (`Mage::app()->getStores()`)
- The Front Controller Instance (`Mage::app()->getFrontController()`)
- The layout object (`Mage::app()->getLayout()`)

Consider `core/app` more of a stateful object then the static `Mage` class, even though that distinction isn't 100% accurate.

After `Mage_Core_Model_App` is instantiated, the first thing that it does is register the Magento error handler and set the default time zone.

This happens within the method `Mage_Core_Model_App::_initEnvironment()`.

The Magento error handler `mageCoreErrorHandler()` can be found in the file *app/code/core/Mage/Core/functions.php*, which is included directly by *app/Mage.php*.

The Configuration Load Process

Since Magento is a configuration based framework (in contrast to convention based frameworks), almost every feature - core or custom - starts with the configuration XML.

---

[1]Please have a look at the source code of the methods `Mage::register()`, `Mage::registry()` and `Mage::unregister()` for details on the Magento registry.

At runtime the XML files are loaded into Magento into a DOM-tree[2] like object structure.

Let's inspect how the config DOM is created, what aspects to keep in mind when working with it, and how to use it to our advantage.

Lets get back to the configuration load process.

The configuration model is assigned using the method
`self::_setConfigModel($options);`.

The `$options` argument seen in the next code block is passed to `Mage::run()` or `Mage::app()` as an optional third argument.

```
protected static function _setConfigModel($options = array())
{
    if (
        isset($options['config_model']) && class_exists($options['config_model'])
    ) {
        $alternativeConfigModelName = $options['config_model'];
        unset($options['config_model']);
        $alternativeConfigModel = new $alternativeConfigModelName($options);
    } else {
        $alternativeConfigModel = null;
    }

    if (
        !is_null($alternativeConfigModel) &&
         ($alternativeConfigModel instanceof Mage_Core_Model_Config)
    ) {
        self::$_config = $alternativeConfigModel;
    } else {
        self::$_config = new Mage_Core_Model_Config($options);
    }
}
```

The code block reveals that an alternative configuration model can be specified in the `$options` array.

This can be used to customize Magento to a very high degree, for example to utilize a different directory structure than the normal Magento folder hierarchy.

---

[2]DOM is an acronym for Document Object Model.

Using an alternative config model also is a technique used by test framework integrations to provide a way to mock models and resource models.

The norm however is that no custom config model is specified, in which case the default config model `Mage_Core_Model_Config` will used.

After the configuration model is assigned, the `Mage` class delegates to `Mage_Core_Model_App`.

The most important next steps are the same, regardless if `Mage::run()` or `Mage::app()` was used to fire up Magento.

First, a custom error handler is registered, before a reference to the config model is set on the `core/app` instance.

From this point onward calling `Mage::getConfig()` or `Mage::app()->getConfig()` will return the same instance.

Note that currently the configuration object still is "empty". No XML has been loaded yet.

Loading of the Base Configuration

The actual loading of the configuration begins next, when **`$this->_config->loadBase();`** is called by `core/app`.
Note the following `loadBase()` method belongs to the `core/config` class, not `core/app`.

```
public function loadBase()
{
    $etcDir = $this->getOptions()->getEtcDir();
    $files = glob($etcDir.DS.'*.xml');
    $this->loadFile(current($files));
    while ($file = next($files)) {
        $merge = clone $this->_prototype;
        $merge->loadFile($file);
        $this->extend($merge);
    }
    if (in_array($etcDir.DS.'local.xml', $files)) {
        $this->_isLocalConfigLoaded = true;
    }
    return $this;
}
```

The method loads all XML files in the *app/etc/* directory in alphabetical order.

All the files are listed in the following table (unless of course custom XML files where added there).

File	Edition	Contents
app/etc/config.xml	CE and EE	A "bootstrap" configuration skeleton
app/etc/enterprise.xml	EE only	FPC Request Processor and Cache Settings
app/etc/local.xml	CE and EE	DB Credentials and adminhtml frontName

Table 8.2: XML files in the *app/etc* directory

Additional custom XML files can be added, but be aware that they are not cached and will be parsed and merged on each request.

The most interesting part of the `loadBase()` method above are the lines inside the **while** loop.

Each file is loaded using a `Mage_Core_Model_Config_Base` instance cloned from `$this->_prototype`.

The `core/config_base` class uses the PHP function `simplexml_load_string()` to parse the file contents, converting each node into a `Mage_Core_Model_Config_Element` instance along the way.

The `Mage_Core_Model_Config_Element` class is a small wrapper for `Varien_Simplexml_Element`, which in turn extends from the native PHP class `SimpleXMLElement`.

Then the loaded nodes are merged into the main DOM tree using the `extend()` method.

The `extend()` method takes an optional second parameter - `$overwrite` - which defaults to **true**.
This refers to existing node values, which will be overwritten by nodes at the same position during the merge.

This is the basis of the Magento configuration load process.

New DOM node children are added to the existing XML tree structure during the merging.

Existing DOM node values are overwritten in case a file that is loaded later contains the same node structure with a different value.

For example, let's assume the first XML file which is loaded contains the following nodes:

```
<config>
    <modules>
        <Meeting02_ExampleXml>
            <active>true</active>
            <codePool>local</codePool>
        </Meeting02_ExampleXml>
    </modules>
</config>
```

Now also assume the second XML file to be loaded looks as follows:

```
<config>
    <modules>
        <Meeting02_ExampleXml>
            <version>0.1.0</version>
        </Meeting02_ExampleXml>
    </modules>
</config>
```

Once the two files are merged, the resulting DOM structure would be this:

```
<config>
    <modules>
        <Meeting02_ExampleXml>
            <active>true</active>
            <codePool>local</codePool>
            <version>0.1.0</version>
        </Meeting02_ExampleXml>
    </modules>
</config>
```

The new <version> node is added to the existing DOM structure.

Now, assume the following file is loaded next:

```
<config>
    <modules>
        <Meeting02_ExampleXml>
            <active>false</active>
        </Meeting02_ExampleXml>
    </modules>
</config>
```

After the merging the DOM structure looks as follows:

```
<config>
    <modules>
        <Meeting02_ExampleXml>
            <active>false</active>
            <codePool>local</codePool>
            <version>0.1.0</version>
        </Meeting02_ExampleXml>
    </modules>
</config>
```

Notice the value of the `<active>` node now is `false`.

To reiterate: the values of existing nodes are replaced, new XML nodes are inserted as new children.

Understanding this is one of the main steps to mastering the Magento framework.

This behavior is also the reason why **the load order** of XML files is very important.

Any file may overwrite values defined in config files that are loaded earlier.

Now that we have an understanding of the nature of the XML merging process, we can focus on the order of XML files that are loaded.

After all the XML files in the *app/etc/* directory are merged, the Magento cache is initialized by the `core/app` model.
This can't be done earlier, since the cache configuration only just was loaded with the base configuration.

As noted before, a consequence of this is that the merging of the base XML files happens on every request - regardless if the config cache is turned on or off.

The exact methods which are used to complete the loading of the configuration differ slightly, depending on whether `Mage::run()` or `Mage::app()` was called to initializing the runtime environment.

However, the order of the following next steps regarding the loading of the configuration are the same:

#	Method	Comment
1	`$this->_config->loadModulesCache()`	The following steps only happen if the cache can't be loaded.
2	`$this->_config->loadModules()`	
3	`$this->_config->loadDb()`	
4	`$this->_config->saveCache()`	

Table 8.3: Module configuration load process

On a side note, between step 2 and 3 listed in the table above, `Mage_Core_Model_Resource_Setup::applyAllUpdates()` is called.

This is an important part of the Magento initialization process, however it doesn't directly influence the configuration load process.

More details about install and upgrade scripts will be covered in the third book of this series: ORM and Setup Scripts.

Our next step is to have a closer look at the methods `loadModules()` and `loadDb()` (line 2 and 3 in the table above).[3]

Loading of the Module Registry

Every module that is known to Magento should be registered in an XML file in the *app/etc/modules* directory.

The method `Mage_Core_Model_Config::loadModules()` delegates to `$this->_loadDeclaredModules()` in order to process those registry files.

That method does so by

a) loading all XML files in *app/etc/modules*

---

[3]The details of the config XML caching are beyond the scope of this chapter.

b) sorting all declared modules according to their dependencies

c) merging the result into the main configuration DOM

The list of files to do step a) is retrieved from the method _getDeclaredModuleFiles().

It sorts the list of files in *app/etc/modules* into three lists:

```
foreach ($moduleFiles as $v) {
    $name = explode(DIRECTORY_SEPARATOR, $v);
    $name = substr($name[count($name) - 1], 0, -4);

    if ($name == 'Mage_All') {
        $collectModuleFiles['base'][] = $v;
    } else if (substr($name, 0, 5) == 'Mage_') {
        $collectModuleFiles['mage'][] = $v;
    } else {
        $collectModuleFiles['custom'][] = $v;
    }
}
```

The base list only contains the file *Mage_All.xml*.

The mage list contains all files besides *Mage_All.xml* that start with Mage_.

The custom list contains all other files in alphabetical order.

The further loading and merging of these files will happen in this order.

This means that any extension can overwrite values from the files starting with Mage_.

Notice that modules from the Enterprise namespace are treated just like other regular extensions and are included in the custom list.

Every extension that should be active during the Magento process is required to have an XML file in the module registry.

By convention the module namespace and name separated by an underscore should be used for the file name.

Some developers have taken to the bad habit of using a single registry file for multiple modules (following the example given by the file *Mage_All.xml*).

This goes against best practice since it offers no real benefit except being less open to modification, less transparent, and also breaks modularity.

The registry files should contain only the minimal amount of information required for Magento to load the main module configuration.

That minimal information is:

- The module's namespace and name.
- The module's activation state
- The module's code pool
- The module's dependencies (optional)

The registration files should not contain any other information, even if it seems related beacuse of a similar XML path.

For example, leave out a module's **<version>** - that belongs into the modules *etc/config.xml* file.

Here is an example of a module registry file:

```xml
<?xml version="1.0"?>
<config>
    <modules>
        <Meeting02_RewriteOrder>
            <active>true</active>
            <codePool>local</codePool>
            <depends>
                <Mage_Core/>
                <Mage_Sales/>
            </depends>
        </Meeting02_RewriteOrder>
    </modules>
</config>
```

When the registry files are loaded, the contents are first merged into a separate DOM structure.

The module list will be added to the main configuration DOM soon, but first `_sortModuleDepends()` is used to create a sorted list based on module dependencies.

If a dependency can't be satisfied because a depended on module is missing or inactive, Magento chickens out with an exception.[4]

After the list of modules is sorted, it is used to append each module to the main XML DOM structure in the correct order:

```
$sortedConfig->getNode('modules')->appendChild($node);
```

---

[4] Yes, circular module dependencies are caught and Magento throws the unsatisfied dependency exception, too.

Loading of the Module Configuration

The loading of the modules' *config.xml* files is often referred to as *module initialization*. It means that a module's configuration is merged into the main config DOM.

Now that Magento knows which modules to initialize, and the order in which to do it, the `core/config` method `loadModulesConfiguration()` is called.

This method can be used to load an arbitrary XML file from every module's *etc/* directory. It's not only used for the *etc/config.xml* files, but also for every other file in that directory, for example *adminhtml.xml* or *system.xml*.

It can also be used to load and merge custom XML files.

For example, the extension Firegento_GridControl[5] uses the method `loadModulesConfiguration()` to load a custom configuration file called *gridcontrol.xml* from every module.

It is commonly believed by many module developers that extensions are loaded in alphabetical order. However, this is not true.

Only extension **registry files** are loaded in alphabetical order. The more important **module *config.xml*** files load order is determined by module dependencies.

The *config.xml* files of modules depended upon are merged before the depending module is loaded.

So modules are not really loaded in alphabetical order. If they are, it's just a coincidence.

Remember, the reason it is important to know the module load order is because through the merge process a module can overwrite configuration values from any module that was loaded earlier.

Magento Trivia

The following is a feature that isn't used by the core, and so far I haven't encountered it being used in any third party project either.

Configuration XML nodes can be forced to extend another existing node besides the parent by specifying an `extends="the/x/path"` argument.

---
[5]https://github.com/magento-hackathon/GridControl

This has no benefit over using normal nesting in XML, except maybe avoiding code duplication.

For further information have a look at the method
`Varien_Simplexml_Config::applyExtends()`.
It is called from `Mage_Core_Model_Config::loadModules()`.

Loading local.xml - again

After all modules are loaded, the contents of the *local.xml* file are merged into the configuration DOM a second time.

This happens so that no module is able to overwrite values declared in *local.xml*.

Another way to say it is that the contents of *local.xml* have a higher priority than any module configuration file.

Loading of the Database Configuration

At this point during the Magento initialization all XML files have been merged into the config DOM structure.

The things missing are the system configuration settings which are stored in the `core_config_data` table.

To add these settings to the other configuration, the `core/config` model's `loadDb()` method delegates to the resource model's
`$this->getResource()->loadToXml($this)` method.

This method has 120 lines of code, but fortunately it is easy to read.

Let's have a look at the table structure to provide a little context for the next section.

Field	Type	Content
config_id	int(10) unsigned	Auto Increment Primary Key
scope	varchar(8)	`default`, `websites` or `stores`
scope_id	int(11)	0 for `default` scope, otherwise

Field	Type	Content
		the numeric website or store ID
path	varchar(255)	XML config path
value	text	configuration value

Table 8.4: Database table `core_config_data` columns

The `loadToXml()` method loads all records from the table and then does some multi-pass processing to merge the values into the configuration DOM.

The steps it takes are as follows.

First it copies all `default` scope records to the `default` configuration branch.

Let's have a look at an example.

The following record

scope	scope_id	path	value
default	0	contacts/contacts/enabled	1

would be added to the configuration DOM like this:

```
<config>
    <default>
        <contacts>
            <contacts>
                <enabled>1</enabled>
            </contacts>
        </contacts>
    </default>
</config>
```

The next processing step are the website scope settings.

All settings from the `default` node of the main configuration DOM - including the data from the XML files as well as the `default` values from the database table - are copied to a branch under `websites`.

This happens once for each website in Magento.

To continue the previous example, assuming two websites with the codes `base_website` and `wholesale_website` exist in a shop, the DOM structure is extended in the following way:

```
<config>
    <websites>
        <base_website>
            <contacts>
                <contacts>
                    <enabled>1</enabled>
                </contacts>
            </contacts>
        </base_website>
        <wholesale_website>
            <contacts>
                <contacts>
                    <enabled>1</enabled>
                </contacts>
            </contacts>
        </wholesale_website>
    </websites>
</config>
```

If this is looking like data duplication to you, you are absolutely right.
But this is only the beginning. . .

The next step is that all `websites` scope records from the `core_config_data` table are merged into the config DOM, into each matching website branch.

After this, all the website scope DOM branches contain all settings from the `default` scope, which might have been changed or amended by the `websites` scope values from the database.

All these values are now copied into each store view scope under the `stores` branch of the config DOM, similar to the `websites` branch.

Every default setting now is present once under **<default>**, once for each website under **<websites>**, and once for each store under **<stores>**

Finally, all the `stores` scope values from the `core_config_data` table are added to each matching `stores` branch of the config DOM.

In the end, each store branch contains a full set of configuration values that are valid for its scope, regardless which scope the setting was specified on.

These are the values that are accessed when `getConfig()` is called on a store model.

Please refer to the Scoped Configuration Values section of the previous chapter for details.

It's good to remember that most of the configuration merging is bypassed when the configuration cache is turned on.

That not only saves Magento from having to read and parse many XML files, but also Magento will only load the configuration sections that are actually used, which reduces the memory footprint quite a bit.

Configuration XML Load Order Summary

The details can always be looked up in the core, but in many situations it is helpful to be aware of the basic load order of all the parts that make up the configuration XML.

The load order is so important because:

- Parts that are loaded later can overwrite node values from parts that where loaded earlier
- Observers are processed in module load order
- The processing order of layout XML instructions within one update handle are defined by module load order
- Module load order can help resolving rewrite conflicts

Remember, the module load order can be influenced through module dependencies.

The load order of the different configuration parts is listed in the following table:

#	Source	Cached?	Mage_Core_Model_Config Method
1	*app/etc/*.xml*	No	`loadBase()`
			`loadModules()` delegates to
2	*app/etc/modules/Mage_All.xml*	Yes	`_loadDeclaredModules()`

#	Source	Cached?	Mage_Core_Model_Config Method
3	*app/etc/modules/Mage_ *.xml*	Yes	_loadDeclaredModules()
4	*app/etc/modules/*.xml*	Yes	_loadDeclaredModules()
5	Module *etc/config.xml* files	Yes	loadModules()
6	*app/etc/local.xml*	Yes	loadModules() (again)
7	The core_config_data table	Yes	loadDb() delegates to getResource()->loadToXml()

Table 8.6: Configuration load order

The Magento Dispatch Process overview

So far this book covered the following aspects of the dispatch process:

- Configuration loading (in this chapter)
- The Front Controller (in the Redirect to / chapter)
- The routing process (in the Custom frontend controller chapter)

One important part of the dispatch process that hasn't been covered yet is the view layer (the V in MVC).

The details of the rendering process will be discussed in detail in the next book of this series: Rendering and Widgets.

Let's have a high level look at the main PHP classes used, so the diagram for this exercise can be completed: the *layout* and the *layout update* models.

The Magento view layer usually is initialized when **$this->loadLayout()** is called from within the context of an action controller.

```
public function loadLayout(
    $handles = null, $generateBlocks = true, $generateXml = true
)
{
```

```
// if handles were specified in arguments load them first
if (false!==$handles && ''!==$handles) {
    $this->getLayout()->getUpdate()->addHandle(
        $handles ? $handles : 'default'
    );
}

// add default layout handles for this action
$this->addActionLayoutHandles();

// ...
```

The layout object returned by `$this->getLayout()` is instantiated using `Mage::getSingleton('core/layout')`.

The *layout* object's main responsibility is to manage the block class instances created for rendering.

The *layout update* model `Mage_Core_Model_Layout_Update` is responsible for loading the view configuration from the merged layout XML files.

To render the instantiated block classes, usually the method `$this->renderLayout()` is called from within an action controller.

The generated HTML output is then assigned to the response object's content body.

To see the details of this part of the dispatch process please refer to the core methods mentioned.

The final step in the dispatch process is handled by the Front Controller: it instructs the response object to send the response header and body to the browser.

```
$this->getResponse()->sendResponse();
```

Now that the most important parts of the Magento dispatch process have been discussed, it's time to move on to the solution.

Solution

The diagram lists the most important classes during the dispatch process:

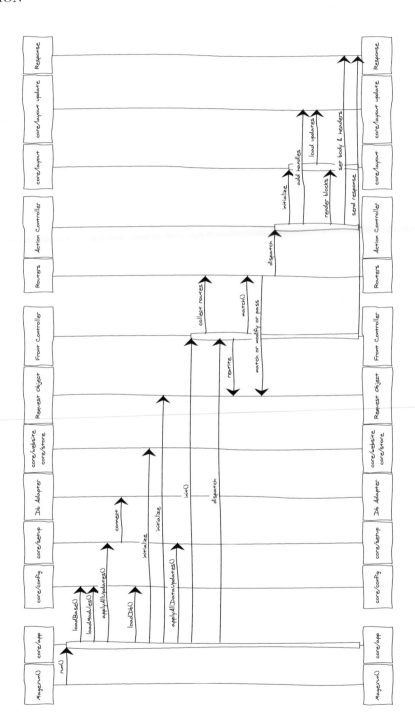

Figure 8.1: The Magento Dispatch Process

- `Mage`
- `Mage_Core_Model_App`
- `Mage_Core_Model_Config`
- `Mage_Core_Model_Resource_Setup`
- `Varien_Db_Adapter_Pdo_Mysql`
- `Mage_Core_Model_Website`
- `Mage_Core_Model_Store`
- `Mage_Core_Controller_Request_Http`
- `Mage_Core_Controller_Varien_Front`
- `Mage_Core_Controller_Varien_Router_Standard`
  (actually, all the routers)
- `Mage_Core_Controller_Varien_Action`
  (actually, the concrete action controller handling the request)
- `Mage_Core_Model_Layout`
- `Mage_Core_Model_Layout_Update`
- `Mage_Core_Controller_Response_Http`

Of course there are many more classes involved while a request is being processed.

Some of them might arguably belong in the sequence displayed in the diagram (for example the session initialization).

However, in some cases the place where a class is used for the first time might vary depending on which page is requested, which modules are installed, or how Magento is initialized.

A senior Magento developer should know the classes listed above and the role they play during the dispatch process.

The ability to create a process diagram like this helps to identify possible targets for customizations and also during debugging.

Chapter 9

Exercise: Store view selection priorities

The original task description from the study group kit for this exercise is as follows.

> Magento can use several ways to specify the current store view for a given request. List the priority of all the different ways.

Overview

This chapter discusses the following topics in the research section and the examination of the exercise solution:

- The process how the current store view is determined
- Multi-website, multi-domain setups
- Admin store view selection

Scenario

Whenever you need to set up a Magento instance with localized domains for more than one website or store view, it is helpful to know how the store view selection process works.

It's also necessary to be able to build customized store switchers.

Also it can assist in explaining some core behavior that might be considered a bug, and make it easier to create extensions that work well with multi-site instances.

Research

To analyze the store view selection process, we need to start right at the beginning, right before `Mage::run()` is called in the *index.php* file:

```
/* Store or website code */
$mageRunCode = isset($_SERVER['MAGE_RUN_CODE']) ? $_SERVER['MAGE_RUN_CODE'] : '';

/* Run store or run website */
$mageRunType = isset($_SERVER['MAGE_RUN_TYPE']) ? $_SERVER['MAGE_RUN_TYPE'] : 'store';

Mage::run($mageRunCode, $mageRunType);
```

We will get back to the environment variables later.
For now all we need to know is that two arguments are passed to the `run()` method: the run code and the run type.

Let's have a look at what happens with those two arguments inside of `Mage::run()`.

```
public static function run($code = '', $type = 'store', $options = array())
{
    try {
        self::$_app = new Mage_Core_Model_App();

        // ... basic initialization happens here ...

        self::$_app->run(array(
            'scope_code' => $code,
            'scope_type' => $type,
            'options'    => $options,
        ));

        // ... cleanup and exception handling happens here ...
```

As you will have noticed, the code sample above is very abbreviated and only contains the code relevant to the current exercise.

The arguments passed to `Mage::run()` are passed on to `Mage_Core_Model_App::run()` as an array.

There, after the configuration is loaded, the arguments are extracted again and passed to `_initCurrentStore()` like this, as can be seen in the following code block:

```php
public function run($params)
{
    // ... more application setup ...

    $this->_initModules();
    if ($this->_config->isLocalConfigLoaded()) {
        $scopeCode = isset($params['scope_code']) ? $params['scope_code'] : '';
        $scopeType = isset($params['scope_type']) ? $params['scope_type'] : 'store';
        $this->_initCurrentStore($scopeCode, $scopeType);

        // ... even more setup ...

        $this->getFrontController()->dispatch();
    }
}
```

Judging by the method name `_initCurrentStore()` it looks like we are finally getting to the code responsible for the store view selection.

```php
protected function _initCurrentStore($scopeCode, $scopeType)
{
    $this->_initStores();
```

Well, almost. In order to understand the remainder of the `_initCurrentStore()` method, we first have to know what `_initStores()` does.

The main thing that happens in `_initStores()` is that the website, store group and store collections are loaded.

This is when the arrays are populated that are returned by `Mage::app()->getStores()` or `Mage::app()->getWebsites()`.

Also, while iterating over the store collection, the default store is set to the first store with a "truthy" ID value, that is, the first store that isn't the **admin** store view (which always has the hardcoded store ID 0).

```
if (is_null($this->_store) && $store->getId()) {
    $this->_store = $store;
}
```

The same is done for the default website, only in this case it is a property of the
core/website model that specifies which one is the default website.

```
if ($website->getIsDefault()) {
    $this->_website = $website;
}
```

After the _initStores() method completes, any store or website can be fetched from the
preloaded lists using Mage::app()->getStore($code) or Mage::app()->getWebsite($code).

At this time the *default* store and website are set, but the *current store* - that is, the
context for the current request - has not been determined yet.

Let's continue with the _initCurrentStore() method after $this->_initStores() was
called:

```
protected function _initCurrentStore($scopeCode, $scopeType)
{
    $this->_initStores();

    if (empty($scopeCode) && !is_null($this->_website)) {
        $scopeCode = $this->_website->getCode();
        $scopeType = 'website';
    }
    switch ($scopeType) {
        case 'store':
            $this->_currentStore = $scopeCode;
            break;
        case 'group':
            $this->_currentStore = $this->_getStoreByGroup($scopeCode);
            break;
        case 'website':
            $this->_currentStore = $this->_getStoreByWebsite($scopeCode);
            break;
        default:
            $this->throwStoreException();
    }
```

The gist of it is that the current store is set according to the specified **$scopeCode** and **$scopeType**.

However, in an unmodified Magento installation, the **$scopeCode** will be set to an empty string, in which case the scope type and code are set to the default website (see the **if** condition).
Because of that the **switch** condition **case 'website':** will match and the current store will be set to the default website's default store.

At this point, if the scope code was empty, the current store is set to the default value.

If the scope code was set however, the specified store will be set as the current one for the request.

But the _initCurrentStore() method isn't complete yet:

```
if (!empty($this->_currentStore)) {
    $this->_checkCookieStore($scopeType);
    $this->_checkGetStore($scopeType);
}
}
```

The two methods _checkCookieStore() and _checkGetStore() take care of setting the current store to something else then the default, if the current request says so.

First _checkCookieStore() checks for a cookie with the name **store**.
If it is set to a valid store code, **$this->_currentStore** is set to that value.

After that _checkGetStore() checks if **$_GET['___store']** is set to a valid store code.
If yes, it replaces any previous value in **$this->_currentStore**.

The ___store query parameter is used by the Magento store switcher to specify the target store view.

The _checkGetStore() method also contains some additional logic to set the **store** cookie that was read earlier in _checkCookieStore():

```
if ($store->getWebsite()->getDefaultStore()->getId() == $store->getId()) {
    $this->getCookie()->delete(Mage_Core_Model_Store::COOKIE_NAME);
} else {
    $this->getCookie()->set(
        Mage_Core_Model_Store::COOKIE_NAME, $this->_currentStore, true
    );
}
```

If the current store is the default store of the current website, the `store` cookie is deleted.[1]

Otherwise the `store` cookie is set to the current store's code.

Most of the time this works as expected.
That is, it works as expected if the default store of the current website is the same that was specified as the default store for the current request using `MAGE_RUN_CODE`, or if the store cookie or query parameter was present.

However, if a different default store view was specified using the `MAGE_RUN_CODE` environment variable, then unsetting the `store` cookie introduces a bug:

To reproduce the issue, a Magento instance with at least two store views is needed.

For example, let's assume there are two store views with the codes `english` and `french` present.

Further, let's assume there is only a single website. This website's default store view is `english`.

If `Mage::run('', 'store');` is called, and no cookie or query parameter is present, the `english` store view will be rendered.

Now, let's assume the environment variable `MAGE_RUN_CODE` was set to `french`.

In this case Magento will be initialized with the values `Mage::run('french', 'store');`.

The `store` cookie will be set to the value `french`.

So far no problem, the `french` view will be displayed.

But let's play through what happens if the visitor now switches to the `english` store view.

The query parameter `___store=english` will be appended to the request path by the store switcher.

The `english` store will be displayed, despite `MAGE_RUN_CODE` being set to `french`, as it should.

But because the current store now matches the websites default store, the `store` cookie is removed.

---

[1]The only reason to unset the store cookie I can think of is that it might make the configuration of a reverse proxy like varnish a little easier.
Saving bandwidth by removing a few bytes from a HTTP header certainly doesn't qualify as a reason given today's connectivity standards.

If the visitor now clicks on any link, the request will no longer contain the
`___store=english` query parameter, and the value from the `MAGE_RUN_CODE` environment variable will be used again, switching the current store back to `french`.

One way to fix that behavior is to not compare the current store with the websites' default
store, but instead compare the current store with the store specified by `MAGE_RUN_CODE`.

A alternative fix would be to always set the `store` cookie, regardless if it is the default
store view or not.

The latter fix is easy to implement, for example using an observer for the
`controller_front_init_before` event. The former fix however requires a change to the
`Mage_Core_Model_App` core code.

Summary of the core/app store view selection

The following store view selection priorities have become apparent from the code discussed
so far in this chapter:

1. If the `___store` query parameter is set, it will override any other method of setting
   the current store.
2. Otherwise, if present, the `store` cookie value is used.
3. If neither query parameter nor cookie are present, the value of the `MAGE_RUN_CODE`
   environment variable is used to specify the current store.
4. The default store view of the default website is used.

However, the list is not complete yet.

The Store Code in URL Setting

There is one system configuration option which also influences the current store view
selection.
It can be found under *System > Configuration > Web > Url Options > Add Store Code to
Urls*.

The XML config path for that setting is `web/url/use_store`.

If set to *Yes*, all Links will be rendered with the store code directly after the base URL.

For example, assuming the current store code is en and the base URL is *http://mage.example.com/*, then the login page route would be
*http://mage.example.com/**en**/customer/account/login*.

By changing the store code in the request path, the current store views is changed.

Since we haven't encountered this setting while going through the store view selection process within the core/app code, the question arises where this setting is applied.

The answer can be found during the initialization of the request object
Mage_Core_Controller_Request_Http.
The request object is initialized in Mage_Core_Model_App::run().

Right after the code we have dissected so far, after the stores array and the current store are set, **$this->_initRequest()** is called.

The only thing this method does is to call **$this->getRequest()->setPathInfo()** on the request object.

The purpose of the setPathInfo() method is to analyze the current request and extract the request path, so it is available during the routing process.

In that method we can find the following code:

```
if ($this->_canBeStoreCodeInUrl()) {
    $pathParts = explode('/', ltrim($pathInfo, '/'), 2);
    $storeCode = $pathParts[0];

    if (!$this->isDirectAccessFrontendName($storeCode)) {
        $stores = Mage::app()->getStores(true, true);
        if ($storeCode!=='' && isset($stores[$storeCode])) {
            Mage::app()->setCurrentStore($storeCode);
            $pathInfo = '/'.(isset($pathParts[1]) ? $pathParts[1] : '');
        }
        elseif ($storeCode !== '') {
            $this->setActionName('noRoute');
        }
    }
}
```

The outermost **if** branch checks if the store-code-in-url feature is enabled.

If yes, then the first part of the request path is split from the rest, right inside the outer **if** condition.

If the first part is not listed in the configuration under `global/request/direct_front_name` in the configuration (the second `if` branch)[2], and it is a valid store code, then the first part of the request is set as the current store code.

From an architectural point of view, setting the current store view from within the request object breaks the principle of single responsibility.

However, since this code is processed after the `core/app` store view processing takes place, it overrides all previous methods of setting the current store view.

Setting MAGE_RUN_CODE and MAGE_RUN_TYPE

As discussed earlier, the environment variables `MAGE_RUN_CODE` and `MAGE_RUN_TYPE` can be used to specify the default store view to show a visitor.

This enables us to easily set up Magento instances with more than one domain.

The feature can be used to have localized domains for different store views within one single website.

It can also be used to configure Magento to serve completely different websites for different domains, without the visitor knowing that it's a single Magento instance on the backend.

Here is the code from the *index.php* file again:

```
/* Store or website code */
$mageRunCode = isset($_SERVER['MAGE_RUN_CODE']) ? $_SERVER['MAGE_RUN_CODE'] : '';

/* Run store or run website */
$mageRunType = isset($_SERVER['MAGE_RUN_TYPE']) ? $_SERVER['MAGE_RUN_TYPE'] : 'store';

Mage::run($mageRunCode, $mageRunType);
```

As the comments in the code tell us, the run code specifies a store or website code, and the run type has to be set to either `website` or `store`, depending on what was used as the run code.

Since environment variables are used to specify the values, no Magento files need to be modified - not even the *index.php* file.

---

[2] The `global/request/direct_front_name` node lists special front names which are always accessible without the store code, even if the store-code-in-url feature is enabled.
In a native Magento installation it only contains the `api` and `xmlconnect` front names.

The idea is that the variables are set on a webserver level, ideally within the virtual host configuration.

Since most Magento instances are served on Apache, what follows is an example of how the environment variables may be set:

```
# Match www.example.com or example.com
SetEnvIf Host ^(www|)\.example\.com$ MAGE_RUN_CODE=us

# Match any domain ending with .example.co.uk
SetEnvIf Host \.example\.co\.uk$ MAGE_RUN_CODE=en
```

Depending on the requested host name, the environment variable is set to a different value.

For further information on the `SetEnv` and related configuration directives, please refer to the apache documentation[3].

Still a number of tutorials can be found with instructions to set up a multi-website Magento instance using subdirectories and symlinks.

However, just setting the environment variables is a much easier way to configure a multi-domain setup.[4]

The specified domain names also need to be configured in the system configuration within the matching store or website scope under *System > Configuration > Web > Unsecure > Base URL* and *Web > Secure > Base URL*.

The base URL config value is used to render the correct domain name for links on the website.

Of course the `MAGE_RUN_CODE` and `MAGE_RUN_TYPE` variables can be set based on different criteria then the requested domain, too.

A popular choice is to use a geo-ip lookup service to determine the country a visitor is physically located in, and then display the appropriate website.

Another often-used criterion is to read the browser's `Accept-Language` HTTP request header to find the best matching store view.

But since the environment variables have to be set **before** Magento is initialized, this provides us with a little challenge.

---

[3]http://httpd.apache.org/docs/2.2/mod/mod_setenvif.html#SetEnvIfNoCase

[4]The option to specify the default store view using environment variables was introduced in Magento 1.4.

If they can be set on the webserver level - like when matching the requested domain name - it's no problem.

However, conditions like checking more complex HTTP headers or geo-ip lookups are more difficult to set up, since they require additional logic.

The quick and dirty solution would be to introduce a core code hack by adding the required PHP to the *index.php* file before `Mage::run()` is called.

Changing core code however always impacts Magento when it comes time to upgrade.

For that reason, a more elegant solution is to either implement the logic as a custom Apache module, or to use the PHP configuration setting `auto_prepend_file` to always include the code before the *index.php* file is executed.

Magento Trivia

When switching between store views using the built-in Magento store switcher, the `___store` query parameter is used to specify the new store view to display.

If the store-code-in-url feature is enabled, the `___store` query argument is not appended, since the store code already is part of the request path.

Under both circumstances however, Magento also adds the additional query parameter `___from_store` with the value of the previous store code.

Since on first glance it doesn't seem to serve any purpose, it is a very common customization to remove it from the store switcher target URLs.

So why is it added then, if it doesn't do anything?

The `___from_store` query parameter is actually is used in the method `Mage_Core_Model_Url_Rewrite::rewrite()` to check if there is a record matching the current request path for the previous store.

If it does find a match, the visitor is redirected to the new store view's SEO friendly URL for that page.[5]

---

[5] To enable store view scope `url_key` attribute values for products, the Attribute Management page in the Magento backend can be used to change the scope of the attribute.

For categories it is also possible, however the attribute value scope has to be set using a setup script, since the admin interface doesn't allow editing category attribute properties.

More details on EAV attribute scopes and how to change them will be covered in the fourth book of this series: EAV.

This enables Magento to use localized SEO URLs.

For example, a product's `url_key` attribute might be set to *designer-chair* in the `english` store scope, and to *chaise-design* in the `french` store scope.

When switching from the english store scope to the french store scope, the URL */designer-chair.html?___store=french&___from_store=english* is requested.

Because of the `___store` request parameter, the current store is set to `french`.

During request rewrite phase, Magento first checks if it finds a matching rewrite for *designer-chair.html* for the `french` store view.

Since it doesn't find a match, it falls back to the `___from_store` value's store view, `english`.
Now it finds a match for *designer-chair.html*, and also finds that the correct SEO URL for the current `french` store view is *chaise-design.html*.

But instead of directly serving the requested page content, the visitor is redirected to the SEO URL */chaise-design.html*, so he will see the correct localized request path in the browser, without the ugly query parameters any more.

The `french` store view still is set as the current store view because it was set as the `store` cookie value.

The following isn't interesting in regards to becoming certified, however it might be useful while doing project work:

In Magento 1.8 a bug was introduced that breaks this feature.
In the new class `Mage_Core_Model_Url_Rewrite_Request`, the method `_rewriteDb()` tries to match the `___from_store` query parameter value - a store code - against a numeric list of store IDs.

Hopefully it will be fixed again in future releases. In the meantime we have to fix it our selves, or use a prebuilt extension like VinaiKopp_StoreUrlRewrites[6].

The admin store view

There is one special case in regards to store views, and that is the admin interface.

---
[6]https://github.com/Vinai/VinaiKopp_StoreUrlRewrites

The Adminhtml area is treated like the frontend store views.

It has a hardcoded store code and ID, which can be found in the class constants Mage_Core_Model_Store::`ADMIN_CODE` and Mage_Core_Model_App::`ADMIN_STORE_ID` with the values `admin` and 0 respectively.

When the Adminhtml interface is accessed, the current store view is set in a different way.

All backend pages are served by action controllers extending the class Mage_Adminhtml_Controller_Action, which in turn extends from Mage_Core_Controller_Varien_Action.

Amongst other things, the admin page controller implements the method `preDispatch()`, where an event is triggered:

```
Mage::dispatchEvent('adminhtml_controller_action_predispatch_start', array());
```

The `Mage_Adminhtml` module declares an event observer for this event, more specifically the method `bindStore()` of the class `adminhtml/observer`.

The method is very simple. Its only responsibility is to set the current store view to `admin`.

```
public function bindStore()
{
    Mage::app()->setCurrentStore('admin');
}
```

To summarize: whenever an Adminhtml page is accessed, first the regular store selection process takes place.

Then the Admin router matches the request and dispatches the action controller.

The action controller then dispatches the `adminhtml_controller_action_predispatch_start` event, and the configured observer overwrites the previous value for the current store with `admin`.

Solution

After all the research, the solution is rather straight forward.

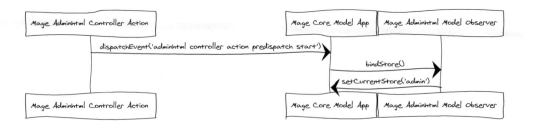

Figure 9.1: Admin Store View Selection

Summary of all store view selection methods

The lower the number in the left column, the higher the priority.

#	Type	Class and Method
1.	Admin area store view	Mage_Adminhtml_Model_Observer::bindStore()
2.	Store code in URL (if enabled)	Mage_Core_Controller_Request_Http::setPathInfo()
3.	`___store` query parameter	Mage_Core_Model_App::_checkGetStore()
4.	`store` cookie	Mage_Core_Model_App::_checkCookieStore()
5.	`MAGE_RUN_CODE` env variable	Mage_Core_Model_App::_initCurrentStore()
6.	Default store of default website	Mage_Core_Model_App::_initCurrentStore()

Table 9.1: List of store view selection methods sorted by priority

Since there is no code to be discussed as part of the solution, this completes the current chapter.

Chapter 10

Addendum

Varien_Object Magic Setters and Getters

The `Varien_Object` class is so basic, we originally decided that understanding this class would be among the reader prerequisites for this book series.

To some degree that is still true.

However, for sake of completeness and to have a place to discuss a few lesser-known features of it, we decided to add this section to the addendum.

All block classes and every model extending `Mage_Core_Model_Abstract` extend from `Varien_Object`.
Often it is used directly, too, as a container object.

The most prominent features of `Varien_Object` are its magic setter and getter implementations.

Through the catch-all method `__call()` implementation, every object inheriting from this class has instant setters and getters.

If you are not familiar with how a call to a magic setter or getter is transformed into a call to `setData()` or `getData()`, it is strongly recommended you open this class right now and read through the implementations of `__call()` and `_underscore()`.[1]

---

[1]For more information on the PHP method `__call()` please refer to the PHP manual[2].

Then come back and read the rest of this section.

What we will discuss here is that the **getData()** methods also offers the possibility to access sub-array records directly.

This handy feature is not known nearly as well as the simple getter and setter methods.

For example, a simple use case of a magic setter and getter would be:

```
$obj->setBackgroundColor('magenta');
```

The equivalent **setData()** call looks like this:

```
$obj->setData('background_color', 'magenta');
```

To retrieve that value, either of the following methods could be used:

```
$obj->getBackgroundColor();
$obj->getData('background_color);
```

Now assume the following setter call is made on a **Varien_Object**:

```
$obj->setColor(array(
    'background' => 'magenta',
    'foreground' => 'lightcyan'
));
```

Lets look at some ways to retrieve the background color again in this case.

The obvious way would be the regular getter methods, returning the array, which then needs to be dereferenced using the correct key:[3]

```
$obj->getColor()['background'];
$obj->getData('color')['background'];
```

However, the getData() method also allows to specify child array records directly:

---

[3]The example uses direct array dereferencing available since PHP 5.4. In older PHP versions the returned array would first have to be assigned to a variable.

```
$obj->getColor('background');
$obj->getData('color/background');
```

If the sub array is nested deeper than one level, the method getData() has to be used directly.
The magic getter only allows access to the first nesting level.

```
$obj->setColor(array(
    'light' => array(
        'background' => 'lightcyan',
        'foreground' => 'orange',
    ),
    'dark' => array(
        'background' => 'cyan',
        'foreground' => 'red',
    )
));
```

```
$obj->getData('color/light/foreground');
```

Using getColor('light/foreground') would return null in this case.

Even though Varien_Object contains many other useful methods, this concludes this section of the book. If you have never done so, it is highly recommended you take the time to read through the available methods.

Class Name Resolution

During hundreds of training hours I've given, one common issue among students is that class instantiation using the Magento factory methods is difficult to debug.

Most students simply start guessing what is wrong, instead of properly thinking things through.

The one way I know to **always** find what is causing the issue is to simply follow the steps Magento takes during class instantiation.

The steps Magento takes during class instantiation for models, helpers, and blocks are exactly the same.
For resource models there are two additional steps involved.

Knowing these steps by heart takes some time, however, it is so worth it.
I have found an astonishing jump in efficiency once I had memorized the XPaths that
Magento uses during class resolution.

If you don't know them like the back of your hand already, to get started, I suggest you
read through the following list of steps.

Then go through two examples. And then, in future, every time an instantiation or rewrite
doesn't immediately work as expected, take this list and go through each step in your
mind.

Using a piece of old fashioned paper can be a helpful tool while doing so.

I guarantee you will find the reason for the unexpected result. And what is even better,
after a while you will automatically make no more mistakes like that any more.

Reading the code of other developers and the core also gets a lot easier.

And finally, to give you one more reason, knowing these steps in detail will help you through
the certification exam, too.

In the examples below I use a factory name of `example/thing`.
This is split by Magento to a *"class group"* "example and a part-after-the-slash *"thing"*.

Please refer to the class rewrites section of the Order Rewrite chapter for more details.

All of the following class name resolution steps are handled inside of the class
`Mage_Core_Model_Config`.

Model Instantiation Steps

The following steps are used whenever a factory name is passed to one of the following
factory methods (that is the class name is specified using the Magento notation with a /):

- `Mage::getModel()`
- `Mage::getSingleton()`
- `Mage::helper()`
- `Mage::app()->getLayout()->createBlock()`

1. Factory method call, example given `Mage::getModel('example/thing')`
2. The factory name is `example/thing`
3. Split into class group `example` and the class suffix `thing`

4. Config XPath lookup: `global/models/example/rewrite/thing`
5. If exists, use as class name; if not, continue
6. Config XPath lookup: `global/models/example/class`
7. If exists, resolves to model **class prefix**, example given `This_Example_Model`
8. Otherwise build class prefix as `'Mage_'` . `'example'` . `'_Model_'` . `'thing'`
9. Append the class suffix, that is, the part of the factory name after the slash
10. Resolves to `This_Example_Model_Thing`
11. Trigger autoloader if class is not known to PHP
12. Resolves to file system path *This/Example/Model/Resource/Thing.php*
13. Include this file and instantiate the class

The most common mistake is that step 6 fails, that is, Magento is unable to resolve the class group to a class prefix.

The best method to start debugging instantiation within the `core/config` instance is `Mage_Core_Model_Config::getGroupedClassName()`.

Resource Model Instantiation Steps

The following steps are used when instantiating resource models or collections.

That is, any class instantiated using `Mage::getResourceModel()` or `Mage::getResourceSingleton()` will use the following steps during class resolution (if a factory name containing a `/` is used to specify the class).

1. Call to factory method, example given `Mage::getResourceModel('example/thing')`
2. The Factory name is `exampel/thing`
3. Split into class group `example` and the class suffix `thing`
4. Config XPath lookup: `global/models/example/resourceModel`
5. Resolves to the *resource class group*, for example `example_resource`
6. Config XPath lookup: `global/models/example_resource/rewrite/thing`
7. If exists, use as class name; if not, continue
8. Config XPath lookup: `global/models/example_resource/deprecatedNode`
9. Resolves to former (pre Magento 1.6) resource class group, example given `example_mysql4`
10. If it exists, config XPath lookup: `global/models/example_mysql4/rewrite/thing`
11. If exists, use as class name. If not continue

12. Config XPath lookup: `global/models/example_resource/class`
13. If exists, resolves to **resource class prefix**, example given `This_Example_Model_Resource`
14. Otherwise build resource class prefix as `'Mage_'` . `'example_resource'` . `'_Model_'` . `'thing'`
15. Append the class suffix, that is, the part of the factory name after the slash
16. Resolves to `This_Example_Model_Resource_Thing`
17. Trigger autoloader if class is not known to PHP
18. Resolves to file system path *This/Example/Model/Resource/Thing.php*
19. Include this file and instantiate the class

Note that the purpose of the `<deprecatedNode>` lookup during step 8 provides backward compatibility for old modules which rewrite resource models using the old, pre-Magento 1.6 resource class group.

The best method to start debugging resource model instantiation within the `core/config` instance is `Mage_Core_Model_Config::getResourceModelClassName()`.

Printed in Great Britain
by Amazon.co.uk, Ltd.,
Marston Gate.